Muay Thai
Advanced Thai Kickboxing Techniques

Muay Thai
Advanced Thai Kickboxing Techniques

Christoph Delp

Frog, Ltd.
Berkeley, California

Photographs: Siam Sport Syndicate, Bangkok: photos cover, 8, 9, 10, 11, 14, 18, 21, 23, 35, 38, 70, 113, 150, 162, 163, 164, 183, 197, 201, 202
Lumpini Stadium: photos 15, 16, 17, 19
Songchai Rattanasuban: photo 20
All other photographs from the archives of Christoph Delp

Any liability of the author and/or the publishing house and its representatives for injuries to life or property is excluded.

Published by Frog, Ltd.
Frog, Ltd. books are distributed by
North Atlantic Books
P.O. Box 12327
Berkeley, California 94712

Cover design by Suzanne Albertson
Book design by Brad Greene
Printed in Singapore
Originally published by Pietsch Verlag, Stuttgart, Germany, 2002

North Atlantic Books' publications are available through most bookstores. For further information, call 800-337-2665 or visit our website at www.northatlanticbooks.com.

Substantial discounts on bulk quantities are available to corporations, professional associations, and other organizations. For details and discount information, contact our special sales department.

Library of Congress Cataloging-in-Publication Data

Delp, Christoph, 1974-
  [Thai-Boxen professional. English]
  Muay Thai : advanced Thai kickboxing techniques / by Christoph Delp.
    p. cm.
  Translated from German.
  Includes bibliographical references.
  ISBN 1-58394-101-0 (pbk.)
  1. Boxing--Thailand. 2. Kickboxing—Thailand. I. Title.
  GV1127.T45D45 2004
  796.815—dc22
                                                          2004002001
                                                              CIP

1 2 3 4 5 6 7 8 9 TWP 08 07 07 06 05 04

I dedicate this book to my family and trainers.

Table of Contents

Preface

I had already been involved in full-contact sports for some years before I decided to travel to Thailand for training in 1995. I went to Maha Sarakham province in the northeast of Thailand to learn Muay Thai. Master Decha accepted me in his camp and invited me to live with his family. Over a period of several months, I was in continuous contact and dialogue with my trainers, Master Decha, Saknipon Pitakavarin, and Kenpet Luksilam, providing me with the opportunity for an intensive study of Muay Thai. During that time, I developed the concept for my first book, *Muay Thai: Kampf and Selbstverteidigung*.

My enthusiasm for Muay Thai, and the affection of the Decha family and their friends, were the reasons for my regular subsequent travels to Thailand for training. I maintain friendly ties with this gym to this very day and have revisited it on a number of occasions. I have also trained for brief periods in many other gyms.

During one of these travels, I got acquainted with Ajaarn Somboon Tapina. He invited me to his camp in Suratthani, where he supported my in-depth studies. I am grateful to him and his wife for welcoming me to stay with them on that occasion and during my following training travels. Ajaarn Somboon Tapina always took the time to answer my questions on the subject of Muay Thai and prepared me successfully for a fight in Thailand.

In addition, I was fortunate to be trained by the several-time champions Apideh Sit Hiran at the Fairtex Gym and Master Chalee at the Muay Thai Institute. (Some biographical notes on these excellent fighters and trainers follow.) At these two camps I also had many good trainers, such as Master Natchaphol, Master Noi, Master Gong, Jakid Fairtex, Kom Fairtex, and Paisitong Jorsambad.

At all camps in Bangkok, in the provinces of Maha Sarakham, Buriram and Suratthani, in Pattaya and Koh Samui, which I visited for training, I always enjoyed a warm welcome and respectful treatment. All my experiences with trainers and athletes at Thai gyms were positive. I am very grateful for the help and assistance given to me for the seven Muay Thai books I have published so far.

Muay Thai is a traditional martial art that developed many centuries ago. Nowadays, it is used for fitness training, competitive sport, and self-defense. The training is meant to improve power, stamina, agility, speed, and coordination. In the long term, a moderate training schedule provides the opportunity to build and maintain fitness.

As a competitive sport, Muay Thai inspires enthusiasm with its hard and spectacular confrontations. In each match, there are five rounds during which the fighters attack at the highest technical level. The efficacy of the Muay Thai techniques is proven in the ring time and again, a painful experience that many fighters from other types of martial art have. The techniques can also be adopted directly for self-defense. Muay Thai simultaneously teaches the fighter how to avoid an opponent's technique and how to counterattack.

Muay Thai, part of the extraordinary cultural heritage of Thailand, should receive the attention it deserves. Muay Thai has given me so much joy; through my books I would like to make a contribution to the public awareness of this martial art.

A heartfelt thank-you to all who have helped me in the preparation of this book, particularly my family, my sister Barbara for the proof, Ajaarn Somboon Tapina, Amnuay Kesbumrung, Chitsanuspong Nittayaros (Master Decha), Songchai Ratanasuban, Colonel Somphob Srisiri, Oliver Glatow, Saengruck Rucksacharoenkul, Daniel Gallus, Menny Ossi, Richard Delp, and the fighters shown in the photographs.

I wish all readers much enjoyment with this book, and hope that Muay Thai will give them as much joy as it gives me.

Photo 1: Author Christoph Delp in front of the Muay Thai Institute, Bangkok, 1999.

Biographical Notes

Christoph Delp, born 1974, 'Diplombetriebswirt' (master of business administration, graduate of managerial economics) and author. Trainer for Muay Thai and fitness.

Trainer education in Thailand from 1995 to 2001, winner of the mandatory Muay Thai fight against a professional Thai athlete, Chumphon, 2001.

Current publications: *Muay Thai: Advanced Techniques* (2004), *Fit für den Strand: Perfektes Bodyforming* (2004), *Muay Thai: Traditionen, Grundlagen, Techniken* (2004), *So kämpfen die Stars* (2003), *Thai-Boxen professional* (2002), *Bodytraining für Zuhause* (2002) and *Thai-Boxen basics* (2001), www.muaythai.de

Trainers

Ajaarn Somboon Tapina. Fighter name: Roongrit Taveesak Born 1940, seventy professional fights, many years listed in the top ten of the Rajadamnern Stadium, approximately one hundred amateur fights in boxing and Muay Thai. Former senior umpire of the Suratthani province and deputy president and professor at the University of Suratthani. He taught in Canada and Australia. Today president of the Muay Thai Martial Arts Academy, Suratthani (www.muaythaitraining.com).

Chitsanupong Nittayaros, Master Decha. Born 1960, 145 fights, many fights as an amateur. Studied sports and graduated in sports and health. Trained many successful Thai fighters and taught in Australia, Greece, Japan, the Philippines, and Brunei.

Chalee Khuntharee, Master Chalee. Fighter name: Pharuhatlek Sitchunthong. Born 1961, 219 professional fights, five-time champion in different weight divisions. He studied sports and graduated in sports and health. Master Chalee is internationally known as former head trainer at the Muay Thai Institute, Bangkok.

Narong Songmanee, Apideh Sit Hiran. Born 1935, approximately three hundred professional fights, seven-time champion, challenger in boxing for the WBA and WBC title. Apideh Sit Hiran is considered a living Muay Thai legend and, to many, he is the best fighter of all time. He is also a very successful trainer and teaches in Thailand at Fairtex Gym, Bangkok.

Performers

The performers shown in the photos are professional Thai boxers. The number of fights cited refer to fights in large stadiums, such as Lumpini, Rajadamnern, and Rangsit.

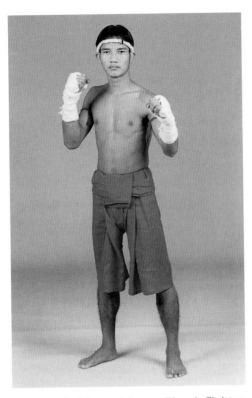

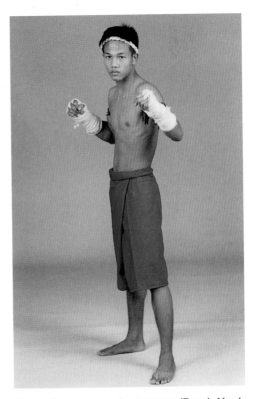

Photo 2: Apichant Jaiprom (Keng). Fighter name: Sakmongkol Sakchalee. Born 1978, eighty professional fights (as of July, 2000), Rangsit Stadium champion.

Photo 3: Mongkon Sermngam (Dom), Yordmongkon Sor. Sermngam. Born 1981, seventy professional fights (as of July, 2000).

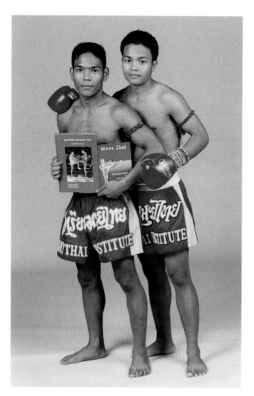

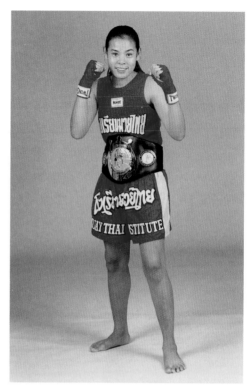

Photo 4: Wanchai Prathumwan (Saeng), Saengpetnoi (left). Born 1976, 105 professional fights (as of July, 2000). Anan Chairum (Kai), Khundet Sor. Sukanya (right). Born 1983, twenty professional fights (as of July, 2000).

Photo 5: Wirun Fongnoon (Roon), Arun Sor. Fongnom. Born 1984, twenty-three professional fights (as of July, 2000), world champion.

Photo 6: Patrick Gayle. Born 1976, professional fighter, actor (e.g. Black Mask II), stuntman. Seven professional fights in Thailand until June 2001 (seven knockouts). Champion Hua Hin province. He is shown in the book Bodytraining für Zuhause (Delp, 2002).

Photo 7: Pai Nakaam (Pai), Singthon Por. Phakaamroen (left). Born 1982, fifteen professional fights (as of June, 2001). Sooksaan Promboot (Saan). Fighter name: Petrangsaan Sitpayak (right). Born 1982, fifty professional fights (as of June, 2001).

Part I

Muay Thai as Competitive Sport

Photo 8: Lukporkoon Por Yodsanan carries out a jumping knee kick.
Winner: Petchawang Aborigine, Lumpini Stadium, 2001.

◊ Chapter 1

Development of the Sport

Muay Thai has been practiced as a competitive sport for many centuries. In the twentieth century, far-reaching changes were implemented, such as construction of boxing stadiums and the use of boxing gloves, which led to increased popularity and international appreciation of this form of martial arts as sport. In recent years, Muay Thai gyms have been opened in many countries, and the number of students has significantly increased. It is currently under discussion what changes are required to establish Muay Thai worldwide.

Audiences in Thailand

The changing interests of Thai audiences are a considerable problem. Only a few decades ago, families of all social classes went to the fights, as the matches were adored as art. To the enjoyment of the spectators, the athletes tried to impress the crowds with a large variety of techniques. The best competitors were heroes and were frequently better known than today's current champions. Professor Somboon Tapina tells of a public festival atmosphere at important fights. Some of the spectators gambled, but this was not the main reason to see the events.

The situation has changed. Now the audience in the stadiums and those watching on TV are mainly interested in betting. The focus is on who wins, not on a large variety of attractive techniques. The amount of money in bets has an influence on the competitors' purse, which is the reason why the competitors do not really attempt to show their technical skills but conduct very hard and energetic fights. Apideh Sit Hiran criticizes this approach, which results in many clinch situations. In his time as an active fighter, the style was more rational, and fighters attempted to seek an early end once the opportunity arose. Other interested parties complain that the athletes are only feeling each other out in the first and second rounds, leading to boring fights for many spectators who are not predominantly interested in gambling.

Photo 9: Paruehatnoi Sitjamee strikes Yordradaap Daopae-drew with a kick. Winner Paruehatnoi, Lumpini Stadium, 2001.

Muay Thai fans are demanding that fights should again be focused on the arts, to the delight of many enthusiastic specta-tors. The fighters are being urged to apply the greatest possible variety of techniques from round one to round five, so that more and more spectators who are interested in the sport, and not in betting, return to the arenas. For such changes to be implemented, the promoters, owners of gyms, and umpires must jointly agree on changes to the scoring system. Once the sport succeeds in attracting the crowds back into the stadium, it will facilitate attempts to establish Muay Thai on an international scale.

Photo 10: Kuntipong Looktup-A-Kart (red) defeats Detpraharn Por Peecha (blue), Lumpini Stadium, 2000.

Amateur Sport in Thailand

The majority of gyms in Thailand are for professional athletes. The respective managers and trainers are entitled to a part of the purse, which is why they try to train their fighters for competition at the earliest opportunity. They equip their gyms with the bare necessities and admit a limited number of athletes for training. Efforts are made to select fighters from poor backgrounds who are motivated to improve their own living conditions and the conditions of their families. Excelling in Muay Thai means leading a very disciplined life. Fighters must be prepared to live in this way. Punters who exert a great influence on professional Muay Thai often visit the gyms.

Well-to-do parents do not wish their children to train at such locations. They are, however, aware of the importance of regular fitness and self-defense training, which is why their children are trained in other types of martial arts. To this end, for example, Tae Kwon Do gyms dedicated to the training of pure amateurs have started to spread in Thailand.

This situation induced the Thai government to promote Muay Thai, as it is part of Thai cultural heritage. The government is now attempting to establish the amateur sport on a large scale, and many control measures for the professional sphere have been initiated. As a result, all social classes are beginning to accept Muay Thai as a martial art again. Gyms financed by their income from amateur training can now be found in Thailand. These are well equipped and maintained, and subject to strict controls. They are open to anybody, regardless of their age, sex, or prior athletic experience. Different courses, in accordance with performance standards, are offered, and the students are presented with a certificate at the end of a course.

Acceptance and International Recognition

Muay Thai enjoys an ever-increasing popularity as a sport and form of self-defense throughout the world. The efficiency of the sport has long been known, but few qualified trainers could be found outside Thailand. Many courses were offered by people whose knowledge was based on a combination of experience in different types of martial art and some fleeting impressions gained by watching assorted Muay Thai videos. In addition, fights without Thai approval featuring competitors at vastly different levels were staged. All this led to negative media reports on Thai boxing. The sport was described as brutal and unregulated, and this was attributed to a certain social class.

Recent years have seen a positive trend due to the Thai government's campaign and the efforts of Muay Thai followers. At the same time, the large number of fitness programs with martial art elements led to social acceptance and appreciation of Thai boxing. Many Thai boxing courses are now being offered, and new gyms with Thai trainers have opened.

For this reason the performance level of fights outside Thailand has improved considerably. They can no longer be compared to the fights staged some years ago, which frequently could not satisfy the organization and quality requirements of Muay Thai. Nevertheless, many such fights are still carried out beyond the limits of Thai regulation.

In the future, the representatives and promoters of the sport must cooperate and present a common picture of Muay Thai. They must coordinate their efforts with officials in the areas of martial art and fitness. Rules and regulations must be coordinated and comprehensive trainer education should be introduced. If all this is done, Muay Thai could be established internationally and even become an Olympic competition, like other types of martial art.

Photo 11: Vichan Ponlarit, Fighter name: Srisatchanalai Sasriprapayin, Born: 1976, Home town: Sukhothai province, Approx. 127 professional fights (as of June, 2001), Former Rajadamnern champion, Olympic flyweight boxing champion (Sydney, 2000), He finished his active career after the win at the Olympic Games.

Muay Thai as Fitness Exercise

Numerous fitness programs with martial art elements have been pushing their way onto the market since the mid-nineties. The courses are frequently booked up and attended by celebrities such as Jennifer Lopez, Carmen Electra, and Brooke Shields. These programs have furthered the public awareness of the positive influence of martial arts on elements of physical fitness, such as agility, strength, stamina, and coordination (see Delp, 2002).

Many of those who founded the various contact-sport aerobic courses now take each other to court in order to maintain and strengthen their market position. However, disputes regarding who copied who are often dubious. Often a former boxer or Tae Kwon Do fighter, in order to market himself better, will allow himself to be depicted in Thai boxing shorts and offer courses

Photo 12: Ajaarn Somboon Tapina and Niyom Lagsanapang, Suratthani, 2000.

with elbow strikes and knee strikes, claiming that these techniques were taken from his original fighting art.

In fact, similar programs have been on the market for many years, albeit without any large advertising budgets. As Master Decha reports, he had taught Muay Thai with aerobic elements since the mid-eighties. At the time, he conducted such courses with a large number of participants in Australia, but these classes were never marketed extensively under a common name.

The different fitness programs include Muay Thai techniques because of their proven efficacy and daily use in Thai boxing rings. Muay Thai's potential has not yet been exhausted to its fullest, at least not under the name of Muay Thai. Muay Thai itself is useful as training for fitness, self-defense, and competition. The sport must become more open and react to trends and requirements. For example, programs with effective Thai boxing techniques could be offered as "Muay Thai Aerobics" or "Muay Thai Bag Workout." Thai boxing training can be a very sensible alternative fitness exercise for individual and group training. Students wearing pads can practice a great number of effective techniques on moving targets and lose weight in the process.

Excerpts from an Interview with Niyom Lagsanapang

Under his fighting names Niyom Sit Hiran and Niyom Ratanasit, Niyom Lagsanapang appeared in more than three hundred professional fights. He has been a several-time Thai champion and the best international fighter in his section. In addition, he was listed among the best Thai fighters for approximately six years. Particular mention must be made of his fight as Rajadamnern champion versus the Lumpini champion at the time, Rerngchai Srisothorn, which he won by knockout in the first round.

The interview dates back to the year 2000, on the opening of the Muay Thai Martial Arts Academy in Suratthani.

C.D.: Where does your interest in Muay Thai come from and at what age did you start training?

N.L.: The sport was very popular at the time, and I was also fascinated. If I did not have the money to pay for a ticket, I would climb the adjoining trees and watch the fights from there. At the age of twelve, I started with regular training.

C.D.: When did you have your first fight?

N.L.: I had my first fight at the age of ten, without any previous training. A fighter was required at a festival, and I volunteered. I won this particular children's contest and had a nice ring experience, which led me to start with regular training.

C.D.: How many fights did you have and what was your rate of success?

N.L.: I had more than three hundred professional fights and was a two-time champion. In 1954, I defeated Rerngchai Srisothorn, the Lumpini champion at the time, by knockout in the first round.

C.D.: At what age did you finish your career and what did you do thereafter?

N.L.: I had my last fight at thirty-three. Subsequently, I worked for some time as a manager and trainer. However, I did not have the success I had hoped for, so I retired from this profession after a number of years. Thereafter, I opened my own specialty fish shop. Today I am a pensioner.

C.D.: Are you still active in sports?

N.L.: After my active time as fighter, I trained in various types of sport. I am still jogging and regularly ride my bicycle.

C.D.: Are you still watching Muay Thai fights and can you detect changes from your active time?

N.L.: I regularly watch fights and can see many changes. Today's fights are dominated by power instead of using the brain, so fights come to many clinch situations. This is neither attractive to watch nor particularly efficient. Today's purses are much higher than in the past, although we used to have a far bigger audience. There was some betting, though not as much.

C.D.: What do you think of the athletic development of foreigners who enter fights in Thailand?

N.L.: The foreigners are improving. Frequently, I like their style. They apply many different techniques and are particularly well trained in boxing techniques. We have only few good foreign boxers in the lower weight classes. However, the higher the weight class, the more the situation changes in their favor.

C.D.: Did you ever sustain a serious injury during a fight? And what is your physical condition now?

N.L.: I have never incurred a serious injury and I am in good shape even today.

Chapter 2

Rules

Thai boxing is subject to strict rules and regulations, but they may differ slightly from venue to venue. The rules listed here are the most important regulations, as applied in the most prominent international stadiums, in Lumpini and Rajadamnern.

Important Early Rules

Many centuries ago, the length of fights was determined by drilling a tiny hole in the shell of a coconut, which was then placed in a container filled with water. The fight was carried out without any breaks until the shell sank to the bottom. Only a straight knock-out or a technical knockout was considered a win; otherwise the bout ended in a draw.

In the course of a major Muay Thai meeting in Bangkok in 1995, it was extensively discussed if, in former times, fights had been carried out in which contestants had used wax to affix pieces of broken glass to their bandages. No written records exist, only oral tradition, so the question could not be definitively answered. Master Decha assumes that pieces of broken glass were used for confrontations in wars, but not in athletic contests.

Important Current Rules

Weight Divisions

The divisions from featherweight to welterweight are the most popular for Thai audiences, and they include the majority of active fighters. The classification of weight categories throughout Thailand generally corresponds to the regulations of Lumpini Stadium (page 19) and Rajadamnern Stadium (page 23).

The following is a guideline for international classifications. Some associations have slightly different weight divisions.

Weight Class	Weight
Mini flyweight	not over 105 pounds
Junior flyweight	not over 108 pounds
Flyweight	not over 112 pounds
Junior bantamweight	not over 115 pounds
Bantamweight	not over 118 pounds
Junior featherweight	not over 122 pounds
Featherweight	not over 126 pounds
Junior lightweight	not over 130 pounds
Lightweight	not over 135 pounds
Junior welterweight	not over 140 pounds
Welterweight	not over 147 pounds
Junior middleweight	not over 154 pounds
Middleweight	not over 160 pounds
Super middleweight	not over 168 pounds
Light heavyweight	not over 175 pounds
Super light heavyweight	not over 182 pounds
Cruiserweight	not over 190 pounds
Heavyweight	not over 209 pounds
Super heavyweight	over 209 pounds

Equipment

In the categories up to and including the welterweight division, the fights are carried out with 8-ounce boxing gloves. Heavier divisions use 10-ounce gloves.

The athletes must wear Muay Thai shorts of a predetermined design. In addition, an abdomen protector of hard material and a mouth guard must be used. For further protection, elastic bandages around the foot joints are permitted but not prescribed. Amateurs must also use head guard, elbow and body protectors. Some associations prescribe shin guards.

Medical Support

All athletes must undergo regular medical inspections in order to obtain a license for fights. In addition, shortly before a fight, a doctor examines the athletes for injuries. These checkups should also include tests for doping and infectious disease, although this is not always done in Thailand.

During fights, the doctor must be right next to the ring in order to ensure the safety and health of the athletes. If blood is discovered in the eye of a fighter from a cut above the eye or a deep cut elsewhere, the doctor must tell the umpire to stop the fight.

After a knockout, the injured fighter will be suspended for a certain number of weeks. The length of time depends on the type of knockout and possible earlier injuries.

Whai Khru and Ram Muay

Prior to each fight, the athletes perform a Whai Khru and a Ram Muay out of respect for their teacher and their camp. These performances are accompanied by traditional music (see pp. 29-38).

Music

Muay Thai fights have been accompanied by music for many centuries. The orchestra is usually made up of four musicians, although at smaller events the music is usually played by a tape recorder. Such a Muay Thai group should also accompany events outside Thailand, in order to uphold the tradition of the sport.

The music starts as soon as the speaker has announced the Whai Khru and Ram Muay ceremonies and continues until both

Photo 13: Concentration during Whai Khru, Rangsit Stadium, 2000.

fighters have ended their performances. Subsequently, the speaker issues the order for the start of the fight, and the musicians resume playing, now with considerably more vigor.

They endeavor to follow the action in the ring and play slower or faster depending on the action. If the athletic performance turns out to be less than eventful, they play very fast to push the fighters ahead. The musicians cease their playing only during breaks.

Whai Khru and a Ram Muay

Length of the Fight

Professional male fighters have to go through five rounds of three minutes each. Between rounds there is a two-minute break. Professional woman Muay Thai fighters also have to go the distance of five rounds. The rounds are, however, limited to two minutes. The length of amateur fights depends on the promoter and the fight division of the athlete.

Admissible Techniques and Scoring

The opponent can be hit, kicked, and pushed with any parts of the body except the head. In women's fights, using the elbow is forbidden. Otherwise the same regulations apply. Amateurs have different performance levels with a variety of regulations.

Fights are decided by knockout or by the three umpires in accordance with a point system.

In photo 14, the umpire tries to protect the falling Por Sumnunchai. Winner Lumnamoon Sor Sumalee (Lumpini champion and WMTC champion), Thailand, 2000.

Fouls

An attack may not be directed toward the genitals, the back of the body, or the eyes. If the opponent goes down or the umpire intervenes, the technique must be stopped.

Holding on to the ropes or intentionally turning one's back to an opponent is not permitted; neither is tossing opponents with Judo or ringer techniques. Unfair moves, such as biting, spitting, and verbal abuse will be fined in the ring.

Fight violations receive a warning—either a reduction in points or exclusion from the fight—depending on their gravity.

Chapter 3

Stadiums

Thailand has two big arenas: the Lumpini Stadium and the Rajadamnern Stadium. They are the venues for several fights each week. The atmosphere at these events is extraordinary. Thousands of spectators yell and shout to encourage their favorites. Many tourists recall a visit to such an event as an unforgettable experience.

Thailand has many other stadiums, and the Rangsit Stadium deserves special mention. It has developed into the Muay Thai Institute, a training site for national and international athletes.

Lumpini Stadium

The Lumpini Stadium is internationally renowned for its Muay Thai and boxing events. Since December 8, 1956, it has been the venue for regular fights. Before Lumpini Stadium's completion, the Rajadamnern Stadium was the only venue in Bangkok, so athletes had long waits between fights. The Lumpini Stadium was established for the protection of the martial art of Muay Thai and to enable athletes to compete in many fights.

The stadium was also meant improve the chances of success for classical boxers in international competition (for example, at the Olympic Games), thereby honoring Thailand. The stadium is controlled by the army and is also used for army events. The first manager was Lieutenant Colonel Erb Saengrit. He was in charge of the Lumpini Stadium until June 1961 and rapidly established its national reputation for Muay Thai fights and international boxing events.

Lumpini Promoters in June 2001

- Virat Vachirarattanawong (Suek Petyindee program)
- Song Kanjanachoosuk (Suek Jaomangkom program)
- Bunjong Busarakamwong (Suek Fairtex program)
- Sithichai Theeradespong (Suek Kietpet program)
- Wiratana Pai-Anun (Suek Prai Anan program)
- Pramuk Rojanaton (Suek Por Pramook program)

Photo 15 shows Lieutenant General Waanchai Nilkiew, manager of the Lumpini Stadium since October 1, 1998.

Address

Lumpini Boxing Stadium
Rama IV Road, Patumwan, Bangkok
Tel.: 2528765, 2514303

Fight Schedules

Tuesdays	6:00 p.m.
Fridays	6:00 p.m.
Saturdays	5:00 p.m. and 8:30 p.m.

Tickets, depending on the distance to the ring cost, 1000, 500, or 250 Baht.

Lumpini Champions in November 2001

Mini flyweight (not over 105 pounds): Yodsaenglai Petyindee (champion since August 21, 2001)

Junior flyweight (not over 108 pounds): Pornsawan Por Pramook (champion since May 29, 2001)

Flyweight (not over 112 pounds): Thapaothong Euipmentair (champion since August 10, 2001)

Junior bantamweight (not over 115 pounds): Pettapee Liengdonmuang (champion since January 24, 2001)

Bantamweight (not over 118 pounds): Fasuchon Sit-O (champion since July 17, 2001)

Junior featherweight (not over 122 pounds): Saenghiran Lukbunyai (champion since July 17, 2001)

Featherweight (not over 126 pounds): Vacant
Number one challenger: Orono Majesticgym

Junior lightweight (not over 130 pounds): Sumkor Chor Ratchatasupak (champion since April 22, 2000)

Lightweight (not over 135 pounds): Namsaknoi Yoothhakarnkamthorn (champion since April 25, 2000)

Junior welterweight (not over 140 pounds): Chokdee Por Pramook (champion since March 13, 2001)

Welterweight (not over 147 pounds): Vacant
Number one challenger: Nuengkrakarn Por Mueng-Ubon

Photo 16: Yodsaenglai Petyindee, Mini flyweight champion

Photo 17: Pornsawan Por Pramook, Junior flyweight champion

Photo 18: Sumkor Chor Ratchatasupak, Junior lightweight champion

Photo 19: Chokdee Por Pramook, Junior welterweight champion

Rajadamnern Stadium

Next to the Lumpini Stadium, the Rajadamnern Stadium is the best-known arena for Thai boxing contests. Only the best athletes get the opportunity to fight in one of these stadiums.

History

In 1941, the then prime minister of Thailand, Field Marshal P. Pibulsongkram, gave orders for a national boxing stadium. A court on the Rajadamnern Nok Road was chosen for the project and can still be found there today. Construction started on March 1, 1941. During World War Two, work stopped temporarily due to supply shortages. In 1945, the work restarted, and the project was finished in four months. The first fights took place on December 23, 1945. During the following four years, the stadium had no roof. In 1949, a roof was planned. In the course of modernization, which took until 1951, the capacity of the stadium was increased.

In the first seven years after its opening, the stadium was managed by the Royal Representation. During that time the stadium operated at a loss, which is why it was then leased to a Thai firm. The manager at the time, Chalerm Cheosakul, requested permission to continue his work and founded the Rajadamnern Company, Ltd., on May 24, 1953. Ever since then, this firm has operated the Rajadamnern Stadium. Over time, the stadium has become one of the best-known international arenas for Thai boxing and is considered to be a Thai institution.

Address

Rajadamnern Stadium
Rajadamnern Nok Road
Pompab Satroo Pai
10200 Bangkok

Fight Schedules

Mondays	5:00 p.m.
Wednesdays	6:00 p.m.
Thursdays	6:00 p.m.
Sundays	5:00 p.m.

Tickets, depending on the distance to the ring, cost 1000, 500 or 250 Baht.

Rajadamnern Champions in November 2001:

Mini flyweight (not over 105 pounds):
Waanlamyai Sit-Kuan-Im

Junior flyweight (not over 108 pounds):
Pirabkao Por Peeya

Flyweight (not over 112 pounds):
Pongsing Kiatchansing

Junior bantamweight (not over 115 pounds):
Vacant

Bantamweight (not over 118 pounds):
Lertsila Choompaetor

Junior featherweight (not over 122 pounds):
Noompoothai Sor. Waanchat

Featherweight (not over 126 pounds):
Noppakao Sor. Waanchat

Junior lightweight (not over 130 pounds):
Tewaritnoi S.K.V. Gym

Lightweight (not over 135 pounds):
Thepparit Titkuan-Im

Junior welterweight (not over 140 pounds):
Noppadet 2 Choowatthana

Welterweight (not over 147 pounds):
Chanwit Kiat-Tor-Bor-Ubon

Junior middleweight (not over 154 pounds):
Chaowalit Jockygym

Songchai Ratanasuban

Songchai Ratanasuban is the best-known Muay Thai promoter. He became popular by staging events at the Lumpini Stadium, featuring the best fighters with highly interesting contests in his program. He also made it possible to watch the events on television.

In line with his slogan, "Muay-Thai—Thai Heritage—World Heritage," he has promoted the international recognition of Muay Thai. He has organized events in France, the Netherlands, the United States, Morocco, and Japan.

On December 19, 2000, he retired from his post as Lumpini promoter and joined the Rajadamnern Stadium. Previously, the Lumpini Stadium enjoyed a better reputation for Muay Thai, as it had been staging superior events to the ones at Rajadamnern. Following Songchai Ratanasuban's move, the reputations of these legendary stadiums are expected return to comparable standing.

Songchai Ratanasuban (photo 20), born 1946, Chacherngsao province. Promoter at the Rajadamnern Stadium, president of the firm Songchai Promotion, owner of the Muay Thai Stadium in the Chacherngsao province, and a gym.

Photo 21 shows Muay Thai champions promoting a Songchai Ratanasuban event (July 2001). From right to left: Boevy Sor Udomsorn, Pet-Ake Detchoosri, Thongchai Tor. Silachai, Anuwat Kaewsamrit, Ngatoo Antharungroj, Thaweesak Singklongsri, Sayannoi Royalrainbow, Pornsane Sitmonchai, (last person unknown).

Excerpts from an Interview with Songchai Ratanasuban

Songchai Ratanasuban was interviewed by the author at the Rajadamnern Stadium in July 2001.

C.D.: What does Muay Thai mean to you?

S.R.: Muay Thai is part of our Thai heritage. Nobody knows exactly when this type of martial art was created. Documents are available dating back more than four hundred years. I believe, however, that the martial art has existed ever since Thailand came into being. In the past it was employed for protection against enemies.

Muay Thai started to spread internationally approximately twenty years ago. In comparison to all types of martial art, Muay Thai is the most effective. Muay Thai can be used to promote international awareness and the popularity of Thailand.

C.D.: How long have you been interested in Muay Thai?

S.R.: I already liked Muay Thai as a small child. At the age of sixteen, I started to train and had a few fights at events in village festivities. At the age of nineteen, I began to become active as a promoter of Muay Thai contests and was successful. At twenty-four, I moved to Bangkok as promotion assistant for the Lumpini and Rajadamnern Stadiums. I continue as a promoter to this very day.

C.D.: What are the differences in today's fighting styles in comparison to the past?

S.R.: In the past all types of techniques were used in the fights. The fighters were heavier than today, because not so much attention was paid to the weight.

Nowadays the athletic contests are more balanced, as the technical level and the fitness of the fighters are of a similar standard.

C.D.: How did the quality of foreign fighters change?

S.R.: Approximately twenty-five years ago, Thom Hanrick from the Netherlands came with his students to the Chakuriki Gym in Thailand. Without exception, these athletes lost all their fights. Currently, he is a famous promoter in Europe and his athletes compete at a high level. The foreign athletes are taller and, therefore, dominate Thai athletes in the higher weight divisions. The Thai fighters continue their dominance in the lower weight divisions.

C.D.: What are your future plans in Muay Thai?

S.R.: So far, I have organized fights in France, the Netherlands, Australia, and Japan. It is my aim to establish and promote Muay Thai in more countries.

C.D.: Is there something else you would like to tell the readers?

S.R. Read this book on the art of Muay Thai carefully. Muay

Thai is the best way to fight. It is also suitable for self-defense, and regular training will lead to general physical fitness.

Photo 22: Songchai Ratanasuban, Somlruck Khamsing and Christoph Delp, Bangkok, 2002.

Chapter 4

Whai Khru

Whai Khru and Ram Muay are dance ceremonies performed by the athletes prior to Muay Thai contests. It is often mistakenly assumed that these are Buddhist ceremonies. The Thais take much pride in their traditional performances, which have been handed down for centuries. To be courteous, foreign fighters should also perform the Whai Khru and Ram Muay. The following describes, in accordance with the sequence prior to the fight, the initial access to the ring, then the Whai Khru, followed by the Ram Muay. This is the usual procedure, though it may be slightly altered.

Prior to the Start of Whai Khru

On their way to the ring, the Thai boxers may kneel down in front of the ring steps and conduct a Wai. The Wai is a form of greeting. In the process, the hands are held chin high, with the hands above each other and the fingers turned up. In this way, the fighters express their respect for the particular venue at which the fight is carried out. However, nobody is obliged to kneel down at this place. In addition, before they set their foot on the steps, they can exhale through the nose. The steps are then first entered with the foot on the side on which the nostrils were easier to breathe through.

Prior to entering the ring, a Wai must always be performed in front of the rope. This shows respect for the ring and the performances in it. Some of the Thai boxers also believe in a ring spirit they can appease by the Wai. Subsequently, the attendants pull the rope down and the Thai boxers jump across. Some of the fighters pass their hands along the rope before they actually move across.

In the center of the ring a Wai is carried outwards in all four directions of the audience. The fighter bows. This is one way of thanking the spectators for coming to see the fight. From the center of the ring, the fighters return to their corners, where they perform a Wai. The ceremony of entering the ring is then fin-

Photo 23: Somlruck Khamsing performs the Whai Khru, Fighter name: Peemanamlek Sitaran, Born: 1973, home town: Kon Kaen province, Training camp: Jocky Gym, Approximately 250 professional fights (as of June, 2001), Special achievements: Olympic boxing champion (1996), successful actor

ished. The fighters now sit on their chairs and wait until the music for the Whai Khru commences.

Whai Khru Description

Once the orchestra begins to play, the fighters take three steps to the center of the ring, stand still in an upright position, and take a deep breath to calm down.

Tep Pa Nom

Kneel down, put your left instep on the floor and then the right on the sole of the left foot. The upper part of the body is kept upright, and the palms of the hands are held together chest high, with the fingers are pointing upward (photo 24).

Bending to the Floor

Subsequently, bend the upper part of your body forward and initially place the left, then the right, hand on the floor. Thereafter, the upper part of the body returns to its original position. The right hand is raised first. The entire procedure is repeated twice. In the course of the last exercise, remain in the lower position for about twenty seconds and meditate (photo 25). The meditation is meant to show respect for important people and to request their help for a win.

Ta Wai Bang Com

Return to your opening position of Tep Pa Nom, raise your toes, and spread your knees. In the process, remain seated on your heels. Now the arms start to move to the rhythm of the music as follows. First, move the arms back down, turning the hands so that the backs of your hands are ultimately pointing down. Con-

Photo 24

Photo 25

Photo 26

Photo 27

currently, the upper part of your body is stretched forward. Your hands then return in a large circular motion to the chest, so that, at the end of the movements, your hands are next to each other and your thumbs are resting on the chest. At the same time, the upper part of your body is raised again.

Finally, your arms are stretched out and raised, your head slightly retracts, and your thumbs are moved to the forehead (photo 26). The entire exercise is repeated twice.

Ta Patom

One foot will now move to the front to support the weight of the body, and the upper part of the body is bent forward. In the process, the wrists circle around each other (photo 27).

Prom

Subsequently, the rear foot is lifted and the wrists circle around each other three times.

The rear foot will then rest again on the toes, and the weight is shifted to that foot. The front leg will be stretched slightly.

Tep Ni Mit

For the last move, you get up by the rear foot (photo 28) while your wrists circle around each other.

The front foot returns to the floor and the Whai finishes with a bow (photo 29).

Photo 28

Photo 29

Chapter 5

Ram Muay

Ram Muay combines different dance styles with one type of exercise. Through its performance, the fighters honor their trainer and their gym. They concentrate on, and remember, their own skills, tactics, and their trainer's advice. Ram Muay helps the contestants to calm their nerves and mentally prepare for the fight. The exercise is also a form of body stretching.

In earlier days, Muay Thai experts could determine the fighter's home camp from the Ram Muay, as each camp taught a particular exercise. Nowadays, many fighters have their own style, which makes it difficult to determine a camp.

The Ram Muay follows immediately after the end of the Whai Khru. For its performance, a special type of walk is employed for all changes of position, such as the Yaang Sam Khum, which is very popular.

Yaang Sam Khum

First raise the front foot and pull up the toes (photo 30). Now rest the toes on the floor in front of the body and shift the foot to the outside and slightly turn the body. In the final position, the entire foot is resting on the ground and the exercise is repeated with the other foot (photo 31). Continue until the desired position in the ring has been reached.

Variations of Ram Muay

For Ram Muay, the fighters choose a traditional style, combine styles, or create their own show. The best known traditional styles are: Pra Ram Plang Sorn, Hong Hern, Nok Yoong Fhon Hang,

Photo 30

Photo 31

Nok Yoong Ram Pan, Sord Soi Ma La, Pa Yak Pom Gnang, Guang Leaw Long, Sua Lag Hang, and Saw Noi Pra Pang.

Pra Ram Plang Sorn

After the Whai Khru, the athlete moves to the site for the Ram Muay with his or her particular type of walk. The style Pra Ram Plang Sorn is usually started from the center of the ring. Take one step in the direction of your opponent, one step in the direction of the opposite corner, and then turn again with one step toward your opponent. Once the desired position has been reached, stretch your front arm and move your rear arm as if pulling an arrow and releasing it (photo 32).

After the move, put your front foot hard to the ground. Thereafter, hold your leading hand in front of your face and see whether the fictitious arrow has hit its mark (photo 33). Success or failure is expressed by nodding or shaking your head. There is usually an indication of two failures before success is signaled.

During the entire performance, move your body to the rhythm of the music. Proceed with your chosen type of walk to your oppo-

Photo 32

Photo 33

nent and stamp the floor with your front foot three times. Finally, return with your walk to your corner. The Ram Muay has now been concluded.

Nowadays, fighters sometimes indicate weapons other than a bow and arrow. For reasons of tradition, this is not necessarily appreciated by some backers of the sport.

◊ Chapter 6

Professional Training

A successful participation in a Muay Thai contest requires the highest possible degree of physical fitness. It does not suffice to start with a short-term fitness program a few weeks prior to the contest. To maintain physical fitness, regular training is essential, and prior to a fight, the intensity of training should be increased.

The training plan of an ambitious athlete must contain training sessions for stamina and power improvement in addition to the specific Muay Thai exercises.

Photo 34 pictures Menny Ossi, Anthony, Amnuay Kesbumrung, owner of the Muay Thai Institute, and Christoph Delp, Muay Thai Institute, Rangsit Stadium, 2000.

Muay Thai Training

The daily training program teaches the use of body weapons. If the trainer discovers a body weapon that is particularly suitable for a student, the trainer will pay particular attention to its training. In this way, the student will develop a body weapon by which he or she can dominate a fight or even win prematurely.

It is recommended that you practice the body weapons by shadowboxing and with the training equipment and use partner training to learn countertactics by heart. For sparring and clinching, it is important to pick training partners of a similar or even higher level to achieve progress. The aim is not to prove your superiority to your training partner but to jointly learn the application of attacking techniques and countertactics.

Once the athlete knows his or her next opponent, the athlete's training will be tailored to the fight and the training intensity increased. The trainer determines the fight tactics and looks for corresponding countertactics and combinations. If your opponent, for example, excelled with a hard straight punch in earlier fights, particular attention should be paid to the training of high round kicks to the upper arm. In the course of pad training, the trainer will have the athlete carry out kicks again and again from a variety of positions. Furthermore, the repeated use of straight knee and front kicks from the opposite side is advantageous for fighting such an opponent. The athlete must practice the fight tactics until such time as he is using them automatically. For this reason, the sparring partner must simulate the opponent's fight style.

Stamina Training

All sports that can be carried out with controlled intensity are good forms of stamina training, for example, jogging, swimming, bicycling, and skipping. You should train with varying intensity and change the distances and type of sport, so that the stamina training does not become monotonous and your performance level doesn't stagnate.

For improvement of the basic stamina level, training should be carried out at a slow and steady speed over a period of at least 60 minutes. For guidance, try to maintain a pulse rate of 145.

You should also include regular sessions with a pulse of approximately 155. Jogging distances of about 6 miles is well suited to this goal. If you are physically fit, you can cover such a distance with a pulse of 155 in approximately forty-five to forty-eight minutes.

Training in preparation for contests is carried out in intervals. In Muay Thai, you will have brief fight sequences during which the pulse will shoot up. Subsequently, the fighters will tax each other for some time, and the pulse will go down. The interval training will get you used to the high pulse situation but also to a quick lowering of the pulse rate. The lower the pulse is in contests, the less energy used and the fitter and more concentrated you will be during a fight. Basic stamina training is, therefore, essential for a quick lowering of the pulse after physical strain.

Power Training

Muay Thai requires well-trained trunk muscles to be able to take the many hits to that part of the body. Regular exercises are necessary to strengthen the stomach muscles and the muscles in the lower back of your body.

Strong neck muscles are required to lower the impact of hits to the head. These muscles are improved by the intensive training for clinch situations.

Well-balanced training to strengthen all the muscles in your body should not be forgotten. Of particular importance are the bench presses for the intensity of hits and squats for powerful kicks. At the same time, the strengthening of the entire body should not be neglected, as it would increase an athlete's susceptibility to injury due to unbalanced muscle strength.

Photo 35: Samart Thipthamai, fighter name: Samart Payakaroon. Born: 1966, home town: Chachoengsao province. Approximately 175 professional fights, five-time Muay Thai champion, WBC boxing champion. Samart Payakaroon is considered to be one of the best Thai boxers of all time. After his athletic career, he became a very successful singer and actor.

Training Program

An athlete's training program depends on his or her aims and the available time for training. In professional training, all athletes must adhere to an individually tailored program for optimum performance. Thus, no generally applicable plan can be offered here.

Exercises specifically intended for this type of sport enjoy priority. Three intensive sessions during the week will provide good results. In addition, the athlete must include at least one stamina and one strengthening session during the week. If deficits in stamina and strength exist, plan at least one extra session each for the week. Such training intensity, however, is not sufficient to reach a top performance level. If the athlete trains with exercises specific to the sport more often than three times a week, he or she should alternate hard and soft training units daily.

In preparation for a fight, the athlete must perfect specifically developed countertactics but must also continue with the stamina and power training. A few days prior to the fight, the intensity of training is slightly reduced. Sparring is excluded to forego injuries. On the day prior to a fight, fighters usually rest.

Nutrition

Nutrition supplies the body with the required energy and has, thereby, a direct impact on athletic performance. The correct selection of food results in extended fitness and concentration and also shortens the time required for regeneration. Suitable nutritional substances are carbohydrates, fats, proteins, vitamins, minerals, and water.

The majority of the food eaten by an athlete should consist of complex carbohydrates such as noodles, bread, potatoes, and rice. The body digests complex carbohydrates slowly. As a result, these are supplied to the body over a long period of time. Consequently, complex carbohydrates make you feel full for a longer period of time than simple carbohydrates do. An athlete should eat high-quality carbohydrates frequently because of their high vitamin and mineral contents. Abstain from simple carbohydrates commonly found in sweets and soft drinks. These substances are quickly exhausted and lead to ravenous hunger after a short time. Fats are highly concentrated sources of energy. In the Western world people often eat too many fats, resulting in an epidemic of obesity.

Try to keep saturated fatty acids in your diet to a minimum. These fats can be identified by their solid consistency at room temperature, for example butter and bacon fat.

Proteins are the basic building blocks of our bodies. Our skin, muscles, hair, tendons, and ligaments are comprised of protein compounds. The proteins are continuously built up, broken down, and converted within the organism. They are necessary for repairing body cells and building up muscle and the immune system. The body must have a daily supply of proteins for these processes. If this supply is insufficient, the body falls back on protein compounds in the muscles, which can be damaged by this process. Skimmed milk products, such as yogurt and low-fat cottage cheese, are recommended to build up your protein level.

Eat the ripe fruits harvested in your region, as these have a higher nutritional value than fruits shipped for long distances.

A substantial increase in training intensity, possibly combined with reduced food intake for loss of weight prior to a contest, may result in a vitamin deficiency and a lack of minerals, which increases the likelihood of infections and reduces performance level. In this case, it may be necessary to take food supplements. Consult with your doctor, as an unmonitored increase in supplement use may have detrimental effects.

The body regulates its heat by perspiration. The heat is released by the evaporation of sweat on the skin's surface. Training increases the body heat, leading to the release of more sweat. The amount of sweat depends on the intensity of training, ambient temperature, and humidity. The excessive release of sweat in the course of intense athletic performance requires an additional amount of fluids.Drink plenty of liquids. A minimum of 2 liters of mineral water is recommended. Otherwise the body will be in danger of dehydration. Coffee or alcoholic beverages are not appropriate, as they stimulate the excretion of urine.

The need for fluids is enhanced by traveling from a cool climate zone to a warmer zone for sport activities. For example, American and European athletes who train in Thai gyms frequently require more than 8 liters of water per day. Minerals are also secreted along with the sweat. Compensate for this with the intake of mineral water.

Losing Weight

Body weight is reduced by a calorie intake below normal requirements. You will lose weight through a balanced low-fat diet and calorie consumption by sport. The intake of empty calories such as simple sugars (for example, in sweets and lemonade) and saturated fatty acids (sausages) must be cut down. Do not reduce the amount of food, or the body will get used to smaller quantities and will lower its energy consumption. In addition, if the body is not supplied with a sufficient amount of proteins it will start to use muscle proteins. If normal eating habits are resumed after a strict diet, you quickly return to your old weight and may even exceed it on account of the reduced calorie consumption. Approximately 3 to 4 pounds can be lost per month through a healthy diet and plenty of exercise.

For a contest, an athlete may need to lose weight in a short period of time. This lowers the performance level. Losing weight by strong perspiration shortly before the weigh-in has an adverse effect on the athlete, often causing exhaustion and lack of power and concentration. The athlete should not lose more than 2 pounds on the day of a fight.

Generally, the fighting weight should always be maintained. If a fighter must frequently lose too much weight prior to a contest, he or she will find it more and more difficult to return to the optimum weight.

Training in Thailand

Professional Thai boxers adapt their entire lives to success in competition. They usually live in gyms and start serious training in Muay Thai from childhood. The early morning training sessions normally last from 6:00 a.m. to 9:00 a.m. Another three to four hours of training follows in the afternoon. Such an intensive training plan necessitates sufficient time for regeneration, for which a midday rest is compulsory. Western athletes who have other jobs and pursue their professional careers are unable to meet such demands.

Thai athletes compete more often than their Western counterparts, since boxing is their sole source of income. In addition, lots of fights are scheduled in the lower weight divisions, with many interesting contests. Only top Thai fighters or fighters from the welterweight division upward take rest periods of several months, as they have a limited number of potential opponents. This is why you see Thai athletes with records of more than three hundred fights.

Due to the large number of fighters in the lower divisions, each pound of excess body weight is of crucial importance for success. The fighters must always be in top physical condition. Once they have been notified of an upcoming fight, they usually have only a few weeks for preparation. The training will be intensified and, if required, a few pounds lost. If the weight loss is not on target, the last pounds must be "sweated off" on the night preceding the contest. However, the inherent loss of power caused by sweating off weight is frequently a decisive factor in a fight, due to the high performance levels of Thai athletes.

Photo 36: Master Decha (top, third from left) used to own a gym in the Mahasarakham province. Terdkiat Sitteppitak (second from left) and Christoph Delp spent some time at the gym, Decha Gym, 1998.

The following represents a training plan as often experienced by the author in Bangkok and gyms in the northeast of Thailand. Thai athletes are trained in accordance with such or similar programs. Intensive and less intensive training sessions alternate and include "soft" units that very few Western athletes are able to complete.

Morning

	Normal	Before the Fight
Jogging	2–4 miles	4–6 miles
or Skipping	15–20 minutes	20–25 minutes
Boxing exercises with dumbbells	5–10 minutes	5–10 minutes
Shadowboxing	10 minutes	10–20 minutes
Training with punching bags	3–5 rounds	5–7 rounds
Training with pads	3–5 rounds	5–7 rounds
Partner and clinch training	10–20 minutes	15–30 minutes
Power exercises:		
sit-ups	200	300
push-ups	150	250
Stretching and massage		

Afternoon

	Normal	Before the Fight
Skipping	15–20 minutes	20–25 minutes
or Jogging	2–4 miles	4–6 miles
Shadowboxing	10–15 minutes	20–25 minutes
Light sparring (three sessions per week)	10–15 minutes	15–20 minutes
Training on punching bags	3–5 rounds	5–7 rounds
Training on pads	3–5 minutes	5–7 rounds
Partner and clinch training	10–15 minutes	15–20 minutes
Weight training	according to individual training plan	
Stretching and massage		

◐ Chapter 7

Tricks

In a fight, you must always be unpredictable to your opponent. You must continuously feint and apply new techniques. You can disturb your opponent's timing with tricks, provoke him or her, or even achieve a knockout. A front kick to the face, for example, is considered insulting and will be cheered by the audience. As a consequence, a speedy counter can be expected after such a technique. The counter is frequently not well planned, so you can block it and carry out an effective hit.

Competitive tips I have acquired in the course of my travels to Thailand are briefly listed in the following sections. These tricks should be included in your training as a matter of course. Only then can they be applied successfully in contests.

In this context, I would like to extend a special thank-you to Apideh Sit Hiran, one of the best boxers of all time, who has taken much time to transfer his knowledge to me.

Feint and Punch

Start with a front kick to the body by raising your leg slightly. The leg is then quickly returned to the floor. If you succeed in misleading your opponent into dropping his or her cover to some extent, you should carry out a straight punch as you lower your leg. If you feinted the front kick with the right leg, you should also punch from that side. If you feinted with the left, punch from the left.

Feint and Front Kick

Start with a round kick to the leg, change the direction of the kick movement to the top, and apply a front kick. With the ball of your foot, make contact with the opponent's nose, throat, or eye area. For a hard hit or even a knockout, use the rear of the foot. The kick with the front foot is meant to provoke your opponent.

Apideh frequently applied this technique in his fights.

Feint and Round Kick

For this trick, you repeatedly feint the start of a round kick, to which end the hip is slightly turned in and back. This irritates your opponent, forcing your opponent to lose her or his timing for defense. Subsequently, you actually follow up with the round kick.

Photo 37: Christoph Delp and Apideh Sit Hiran during training, Fairtex Gym, 2000.

This trick can be carried out with the front or rear foot. For use of the front foot, you must transfer the weight to the rear leg. This technique can induce your opponent to use one of his or her own weapons, which you, however, should anticipate and be able to counter effectively.

Apideh also showed this technique to perfection in his contests.

Return Strike with Elbow

This technique comes into use after a cutting elbow or hitting-down elbow has missed the head. Supported by a move of the hip, you promptly return the elbow in a direct line and hit your opponent's chin.

If your elbow fails to make contact, your opponent will usually attack, opening up an opportunity for full contact with your return strike. Should he or she not attack after all, you must take a step in your opponent's direction for better impact of the blow.

Front Kick to the Pivot Leg

This technique is aimed at your opponent's pivot leg. Use this technique parallel to an opponent's round kick, when your opponent is unable to defend. Apideh applies this kick with the heel and a lateral position of the foot for a firmer stance. In training sessions, the ball of the foot should be used, as the heel is very hard.

Particularly suitable targets are the inner side of the thigh and the knee. A hard execution of the technique can result in a knockout.

Defense against a Knee Kick

If your opponent uses a straight knee from a distance, you can strike his or her thigh with the tip of your elbow. Subsequently, use this elbow for a hitting-down elbow or an uppercut elbow.

This technique should be employed in clinch situations with great care. If the blow has no particular impact on the opponent, he or she is able to counter with a cutting elbow technique.

Strike with the Shoulder in Clinch Situations

In clinch situations, this technique is used to hit your opponent's chin with your shoulder. To this end, slightly turn in your opponent's direction, bend your front leg, and strike upwards. In the process, your weight is shifted toward your opponent. The power for this technique is generated by the lowering and stretching of the leg, the shifting of weight, and the shoulder move.

Apideh explained that this technique can lead to a premature conclusion of the fight.

Kick with the Heel in Clinch Situations

This technique offers itself in a clinch situation. Kick your opponent's thigh or back with your heel from behind. Your opponent is hardly able to defend against this technique, as it is difficult to see.

Apideh remembers that this can also lead to a knockout.

Strike with the Palm of the Hand

This technique prevents your opponent from executing a clinch grip. If he or she attempts to apply a grip, strike your opponent's chin with the lower part of your palm. In the process, move his or her chin upward and back. For self-defense, the blow can also be aimed to the throat.

Use of the Rope

When retreating under attack, you must avoid the corners of the ring. If you are close to the center of the rope, take one quick step back and use the momentum of the rope for a forward movement. Then carry out an uppercut elbow to your opponent's face. Do not move your elbow upwards, but promptly adopt the final position with your shoulder shifting to the front, whereby your opponent cannot hit your face. The power of the move comes from the rebound of the rope and the use of the hip and shoulder.

As an alternative, use the swing of the rope for a quick half circle to the right or left. You will be in a lateral position to your opponent and able to counter with a round kick. For application of this technique in training, pay attention to properly tightened ropes.

Apideh used to carry out this particular trick perfectly.

Part II

Effective Countertactics

Photo 38: Pettapee Singtai hits the neck of Woothidet Lukprabat.
Winner Pettapee, Lumpini Stadium, 2000.

◑ Chapter 1

Introduction

Countertactics are simultaneously defensive and offensive techniques. The success of an opponent's technique can be avoided by a faster one, or an attack can be first warded off and followed up by a quick counter. In this way, you will deliver an effective blow and ensure that your opponent cannot apply additional techniques.

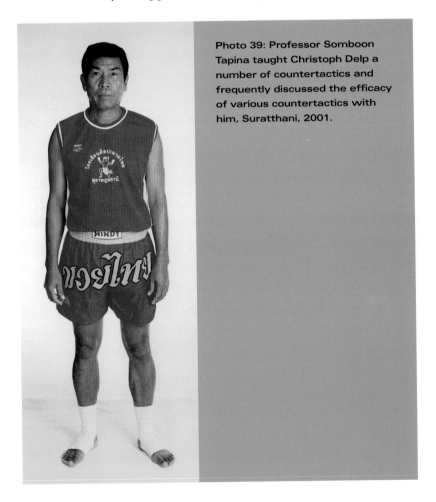

Photo 39: Professor Somboon Tapina taught Christoph Delp a number of countertactics and frequently discussed the efficacy of various countertactics with him, Suratthani, 2001.

After you have gained a certain degree of practice in the basic techniques of defense and attack, you should start to learn some countertactics (see Delp, 2001). This chapter introduces you to some of the most effective countertactics. In contrast, the previous book in this series, Thai Boxing Basics, explains the basic techniques for attack and defense and presents some examples of countertactics.

The selection in the book is based on my experiences and those of famous fighters and personalities in the world of Muay Thai. All trainers and fighters, however, know further techniques that I was able to apply with positive results. These techniques are not necessarily sensible, as their success may be explained, for example, by a very tall and lean body, or extraordinary reflexes.

To become a successful fighter you do not need to master all countertactics. However, the more of these techniques you carry out by instinct, the more difficult it will be for your opponent to foresee your actions. In a contest, use only the countertactics you are truly able to execute with skill. The precondition for the application of these tactics is frequent and regular training. Based on individual characteristics, a fighter may not be successful with a countertactic in competition, despite regular training. For example, an athlete with slow footwork can rarely use the countertactic "step back and punch" in defense of a jab attack.

The following explanations assume that the reader has a leading left hand and is not a southpaw. The reader is taught how to counter all possible attacks in this guard technique. For southpaws, the countertactics must be mirrored.

A detailed account follows on the decisive factors to bear in mind when an opponent approaches and attacks from the left or right side.

○ Chapter 2

Tactics to Counter Punch Techniques

This chapter provides a differentiation in accordance with the opponent's ring stance. Such detailed observation will not be necessary in the following chapters.

Countering a Jab Punch

Counterpunch (Same Stance)

This countertactic is used in defense against a jab, provided the two fighters have the same stance (photo 40).

Catch the jab with the palm of your rear hand, in the process press the thumb firmly into the hollow at the biceps of your punch

Photo 40

Photo 41

arm. At the same time, counter with a jab. The block must be hard, your arm stretched forward, and your weight shifted in the direction of your opponent.

In photo 41, the fighter in the red trunks throws a jab, which is blocked by the fighter in blue.

Step Back and Punch (Same Stance)

This countertactic is used against a jab, provided the two fighters have the same stance.

Take a step back in order to avoid the impact of your opponent's jab. Then, take a step to the front as you deliver a jab to your opponent and transfer your weight toward him or her. Advanced athletes move on the balls of their feet, jump back and forth, and do not change the stance of their legs.

In photos 42 to 44, the red fighter takes a step back before moving forward and countering with a jab.

Photo 42   Photo 43   Photo 44

Lean Back and Punch (Same Stance)

This countertactic is used in defense against a jab, provided both fighters have the same stance.

Lean back so that your opponent's jab misses the target. In the process, your weight is shifted to your rear leg. Promptly counter with a jab and transfer your weight forward for greater impact to the blow. Do not lean back too much, or your opponent may continue jabbing. In addition, your chin must be lowered to your chest to protect your throat.

Photos 45 to 47 show the red fighter leaning back with a subsequent transfer of his weight toward the opponent and the delivery of a jab.

Photo 45   Photo 46   Photo 47

Photo 48   Photo 49

Deflect and Punch (Different Stance)

This countertactic is used against a jab if the opponent's stance is different.

Deflect the jab with the opposite hand to the inside and promptly answer with a jab, using the same arm. To powerfully execute the technique, your weight shifts to the front. Ensure that the blow is pushed away without straining or raising the shoulder so that the move can be carried out quickly.

In photos 48 and 49, the red fighter deflects the jab to the inside and counters with a jab.

Countering a Straight Punch

Lateral Deflection with Step

This countertactic is used in defense against a straight punch. It is not a suitable defense against a jab, as a jab is delivered fast and without too much power.

Take a half turn to the outside to avoid the impact of your opponent's blow. At the same time, push the blow with the opposite hand to the inside. Counter now with a hook to the head or a knee kick to the open side of your opponent's body. A round kick can be used if, with your half turn, you move somewhat further away from your opponent, as shown in the photo.

Photos 50 and 51 show the countertactic against a normal stance. For defense against a southpaw, the red fighter should move to the right and block with the right arm.

Photo 50

Photo 51

Deflect and Punch

This countertactic is used against a straight punch.

Move the opposite hand with a turn of your upper body to the inside. Counter promptly with a punch and turn your chest back for additional impact. Ensure that your body is kept loose and do not deflect your opponent's arm too much to the inside, as you are otherwise unable to make any quick moves.

Photos 52 and 53 show the countertactic versus a southpaw, but it is equally applicable to a normal stance.

Photo 52

Photo 53

Pushing up and Knee Kick

This countertactic is used in a defense against a straight punch.

Block the opponent's technique upwards with the opposite lower arm. Then deliver a knee kick to the unprotected side of your opponent's body while keeping your arm in a raised position.

Photos 54 to 56 show the countertactic against a normal stance. It can also be used against a southpaw.

Photo 54   Photo 55   Photo 56

Uppercut Elbow and Hitting-Down Elbow

This countertactic is used in defense against a straight punch.

For protection against a straight punch, turn the upper part of your body laterally to the front and deliver an uppercut elbow with the opposite arm. In this process, do not deliver the blow from below—as is otherwise usual for the uppercut—but shift the elbow joint shoulder high to the front. Otherwise you will risk being hit. The power in execution derives from the pushing of the shoulder and the impact of the attacking opponent. Subsequently, you can use a hitting-down elbow with the other arm.

In the photos 57 and 58, the author demonstrates the countertactic in defense against Menny Ossi, who has adopted a normal stance. It can also be used against a southpaw.

Photo 57   Photo 58

Front Kick

This countertactic is used in defense against a straight punch.

As soon as you recognize the beginning of a punch, carry out a front kick to your opponent's stomach. For quicker impact, it is best to use the front leg. For this reason, many fighters also use a kick with the ball of the foot in lieu of the straight front kick.

In sequence from the starting position (photo 59), photo 60 shows the countertactic in defense against a normal stance. Photo 61 shows a southpaw.

Photo 59

Photo 60

Photo 61

Turn to the Inside and Punch (Against Southpaws)

This countertactic is used in defense against a straight punch, if you are fighting with a stance different from your opponent.

As soon as you detect the attack, turn your shoulder and the upper part of your body to the inside, so the opponent's technique will miss the target. In the course of this move, carry out a straight punch.

In photo 62, the blue fighter (southpaw) delivers a straight punch. The red fighter protects himself by moving the upper part of his body to the left while simultaneously hitting back with the right arm. Photo 63 shows the technique from a different angle.

Photo 62

Photo 63

Countering an Uppercut

Step Back and Punch

This countertactic is used against an uppercut.

For protection against the opponent's technique, take a step back (photos 64 and 65). To this end, first move your rear foot, followed by your front foot. As an alternative, you may lean back with the upper part of your body and promptly counter with a straight punch (photo 66). For successful application of this countertactic, you must move very quickly, which is why many fighters rest on the balls of their feet.

Photo 64   Photo 65   Photo 66

Countering a Hook

Jab and Block

This countertactic is used in defense against a hook.

As soon as you detect the beginning of your opponent's technique, carry out a straight punch. Concentrate on the rapid execution of your punch and do not tighten the protecting arm. However, if your opponent's technique is initially successful, tighten the muscles in your arm on the side under attack for blocking but continue to carry out a concurrent punch of your own.

Photos 67 and 68 show an attack to the left side of the red fighter, which is why he counters with the right arm. Photo 69 shows the way in which he protects himself against an attack to his right side.

Photo 67

Photo 68

Photo 69

Photo 70: Peerapong Chuanpoe, Fighter name: Boevy Sor. Udomsorn, Born: 1984. Home town: Kalasin province, Training camp: Kietshansing Camp in Bangkok, Approx. ninety-seven professional fights (as of June, 2001), Former Rajadamnern champion (Flyweight)

◊ Chapter 3

Tactics to Counter Elbow Techniques

Counter for all Elbow Techniques

It is better to avoid an opponent's technique or to stop the attack by your own quicker technique than to block. Elbow techniques are, however, carried out from a very short distance, which is why it is frequently only possible to block with the arms held up for protection.

Block and Knee

This countertactic is used in defense against an elbow technique.

Block the opponent's technique with the opposite arm and follow it up with a knee kick to the unprotected side of his or her body.

Photos 71 to 73 show the countertactic in defense against a cutting elbow. As an alternative, the fighter in red could deliver a hitting-down elbow with the right arm after the block.

Photo 71   Photo 72   Photo 73

Step Back and Punch

This countertactic is used in defense against an elbow technique.

For protection against your opponent's attack, take a step back. As an alternative, you can also lean back. Promptly answer with a jab while transferring your weight toward your opponent.

Photos 74 to 76 show the countertactic against a cutting elbow.

Photo 74   Photo 75   Photo 76

Countering an Uppercut Elbow

Lateral Step and Elbow

This countertactic is used in defense against an uppercut elbow.

As soon as you detect the beginning of the technique move to the outside with a half circle so that you confront your opponent sideways. Do not attempt to block in the process. On positioning your front foot, deliver an elbow from above.

In the photos 77 and 78, the fighter in red defends himself against a technique with the right arm. If his opponent delivers a blow with the left arm, the fighter in red must make a half circle to the right and use his right elbow (photo 79). Advanced students position their foot farther to the side, which enables a harder technique.

Photo 77

Photo 78

Photo 79

Countering a Reverse Elbow

Step Forward and Elbow

This countertactic is used against a reverse elbow.

As soon as your opponent starts a turn, take a step forward and strike with your elbow to the back of his or her head. To gain more time for your own technique move the leg forward that is farthest away from your opponent's attack. Make sure that you transfer your weight forward in a straight line. If you move the upper part of your body sideways to the front, you will be slower and the impact of your blow will be reduced. If your opponent's technique succeeds first, block the attack firmly with your raised arm without interrupting your own elbow delivery.

In the photos 80 and 81, the red fighter counters an attack to his right side. For an attack to his left side, he must move the right side of his body forward and deliver the hit with his right elbow (photo 82).

Photo 80   Photo 81   Photo 82

◊ Chapter 4

Tactics to Counter Kick Techniques to the Leg

Counters for All Attacks to the Legs

Jab

This countertactic is used for defense against a leg kick.

Once you recognize the beginning of a kick, take a rapid step forward and deliver a jab at the same time. Your weight must be transferred to the front and your arm must be stretched. In training, strike with the palm of your hand to your partner's chest to avoid injuring your partner.

Photos 83 and 84 show the countertactic against a kick with the right leg. The tactic can also be used against a kick with the left leg.

Photo 83   Photo 84

Front Kick to the Stomach

This countertactic is used for defense against a leg kick.

As soon as you recognize your opponent's technique, carry out a ball-of-the-foot front kick to your opponent's stomach (photos 85 and 86). Regardless of whether your opponent kicks with the right or left leg, it is better to use your front leg for the front kick for quicker impact.

As a result of this countertactic, the opponent loses his or her balance, giving you the opportunity for a subsequent round kick or a knee kick with your rear leg.

Photo 85

Photo 86

Front Kick to the Leg

This countertactic is used for the defense against a leg kick.

Avoid the success of the opponent's technique by delivering a front kick to the middle of his or her thigh (photos 87 and 88). The blow is usually delivered with the front foot. However, to be able to deliver a hard kick for a possible knockout, use the rear end of your foot. The countertactic must then be very quick, as it takes more time to reach the target.

Photo 87

Photo 88

Countering a Kick to the inside of the Front Leg

Pull the Leg Back and Kick

This countertactic is used against a round kick to the inside of the leg.

To avoid the success of your opponent's technique, the leg under attack is pulled back in a half circle (photo 89). To enable a quick move, the straight upper part of your body must also make a swift turn.

Then you should carry out a round kick to the body with your rear leg (photo 90).

Photo 89

Photo 90

Countering a Kick to the Outside of the Leg

Block and Kick

This countertactic should be used exclusively for defense against a round kick to the outside of the leg. It is better to use the countertactics described in the section "Counters for All Attacks to the Legs" (see pages 77-79) , as a block always entails the danger of injury. Sometimes, however, a block is an absolute necessity, which is why it must be practiced in training. As an option, the front leg can be pulled back. This is risky, though, as your opponent may hit your pivot leg.

Block your opponent's kick with the opposite shinbone while keeping your foot and pivot leg stretched (photos 91 and 92). Then briefly return your foot to the floor and promptly answer with a round kick to your opponent's body or head, using the same leg.

Photo 91

Photo 92

◑ Chapter 5

Tactics to Counter High Leg Techniques

Countering All Leg Techniques

Jab

This countertactic is used for the defense against a round kick to the body or head.

As soon as you recognize the beginning of your opponent's technique, take a step forward and deliver a jab at the same time. In the process, shift your weight in the direction of your opponent and stretch your body and arm. In this way, you can hit your opponent hard to the head, so that he or she loses balance and must stop the kick.

Photos 93 and 94 show the countertactic against a kick with the left leg. The tactic can equally be used against a kick with the right leg.

Photo 93

Photo 94

Front Kick to the Stomach

This countertactic is used against a round kick to the body or head.

As soon as you recognize your opponent's technique, quickly hit his or her stomach. The opponent loses balance and the kick is stopped (photos 95 and 96). The countertactic is usually carried out with the front foot. For hard impact, use your rear foot. The countertactic must then be executed swiftly, as it takes more time to hit the target.

Regardless of the distance from your opponent, you then deliver a round kick or a straight knee with your rear leg.

Photo 95

Photo 96

Front Kick to the Leg

This countertactic is used for defense against a round kick to the body or head.

Avoid the success of your opponent's technique by kicking with the sole of your foot to his or her thigh (photos 97 and 98). You can deliver a more forceful kick with your heel, but this increases the risk of slipping. The countertactic is usually carried out with your front foot. For harder impact, you can also use your rear foot. The countertactic must then be carried out very swiftly, as it takes more time to reach the target.

Regardless of your distance from your opponent, you then deliver a round kick or a straight knee with your rear leg.

Photo 97

Photo 98

Sidestep with Punch

This countertactic is used for defense against a round kick to the body or head.

As soon as you recognize your opponent's technique, take a 45-degree step away from the kick to the front. Concurrently, carry out a punch to your opponent's face and shift your weight forward and stretch your arm. By this countertactic, your opponent will lose balance. A forceful execution may lead to a knockout.

In photos 99 and 100, the red fighter counters a kick with the left leg with a lateral left move and a punch with his left arm. For defense against a kick with the right leg, the right foot must be moved forward and the punch must be delivered with the right arm.

Photo 99

Photo 100

Kick to the Leg

This countertactic is used against a round kick to the body or head.

Right after the start of the kick, take a lateral step with your outside leg to the front—away from the kick—and use your inner leg for a kick from behind to the hollow of your opponent's knee. If you want your opponent to fall, you must hit his or her lower leg.

Photos 101 and 102 show the countertactic for defense against a kick with the right leg. For defense against a kick with the left leg, the red fighter must move forward sideways and deliver a kick with his right leg (photo 103).

Photo 101   Photo 102   Photo 103

Countering a Kick to the Body

Deflect and Kick

This countertactic is used against a round kick to the body.

Jump slightly back and deflect your opponent's technique, causing him or her to lose balance. Do not use the opposite hand, as your opponent may otherwise be able to punch your unprotected face. Subsequently, you counter with a kick.

Photos 104 to 106 show the red fighter defending himself against a technique with the right leg and countering with a half-shin half-knee kick. As an alternative, he could aim from the front to his opponent's head or body.

Photo 104   Photo 105   Photo 106

Block and Kick

The block is another method of protection against a round kick. Generally speaking, other defense techniques without contact should be preferred. On some occasions, however, contact cannot be avoided and this technique must also be practiced in training.

For blocking, use the opposite shinbone (photos 107 and 108) and promptly deliver a round kick with this leg. The other leg is only used for blocking (photo 109). A counter from that position is not possible.

Photo 107   **Photo 108**   **Photo 109**

Countering a High Kick

Lean Back and Kick

This countertactic is used against a round kick to the head.

Lean the upper part of your body back, so that your opponent's attack misses its target. The leaning action can also be carried out in combination with a backward step. Subsequently, counter with a straight knee, a half-shin, half-knee kick, or a round kick, for which you normally use your rear leg.

In photos 110 to 112, the fighter in blue kicks with his right leg. The fighter in red leans back and counters with a half-shin half-knee kick. If, in contrast to the photo, your opponent kicks with the left leg, counter toward the hollow of his or her knee.

Photo 110   Photo 111   Photo 112

Photo 113: Thongchai Paktai, Fighter name: Thongchai Tor. Silachai, Born 1971, home town: Nakon Rajchasima province, Approximately 155 professional fights (as of June, 2001), Former Lumpini champion and WMTC champion

◐ Chapter 6

Tactics to Counter Foot Techniques

Countering Foot Techniques to the Body

Deflect

This countertactic is used against a front kick or side kick to the body.

Jump sideways and do not change the distance of your feet from each other. Deflect the kick to the side. If your opponent kicks with his or her left leg, jump to the right and deflect the kick with the wrist of your left hand to the left side. If your opponent kicks with his or her right leg, jump to the left side and deflect the kick with the wrist of your right hand to the right. Depending on your distance to your opponent, counter with a straight punch, a half-shin half-knee kick, or a round kick.

In photos 114 to 116, the fighter in red defends himself against a side kick with the right leg and then answers with a half-shin half-knee kick.

In photos 117 and 118, the fighter in blue carries out a front kick with his left leg. The fighter in red jumps to the right and deflects the kick with the fixed wrist of his left hand to the left. He is now close to his opponent and can counter with a straight punch (photo 119).

Photo 114

Photo 115

Photo 116

Photo 117

Photo 118

Photo 119

Step Back

This countertactic is used for defense against a front kick to the body.

Protect yourself by taking a step back (photos 120 and 121). In addition, bend the upper part of your body back, stretch it upward, and pull in your stomach. You can only counter if your opponent delivers his or her technique with power—to this end, he usually takes the rear leg—and misses the target and loses balance. Then your opponent will be falling somewhat to the front. You must then move sideways to the front and counter, depending on the distance, with a punch, knee kick, or kick (photo 122). If your opponent kicks with his or her right leg, take a lateral move left to the front or, after a kick with the left leg, a lateral move right to the front.

If your opponent's technique is carried out with control there is always the danger that your counter will leave you open for another technique.

Photo 120   **Photo 121**   **Photo 122**

Countering Foot Techniques to the Head

Step Back and Lean Back

This countertactic is used against a front kick to the head.

As soon as you recognize the beginning of your opponent's technique, take a step back (photos 123 and 124). In the process, lean the upper part of your body somewhat back and pull your chin toward your chest to protect your throat. If your opponent delivers his or her technique with force and loses balance when missing, you can counter. Move your leg sideways to the front and carry out a punch, knee kick, or kick, depending on the distance (photo 125). If your opponent kicks with the right leg you move forward to the left or, after a kick with his or her left leg, forward to the right.

If your opponent's technique is carried out with control there is always the danger that your counter will leave you open for another technique.

Photo 123

Photo 124

Photo 125

◐ Chapter 7

Tactics to Counter Knee Techniques

Jab

This countertactic is used against a knee kick from a distance.

As soon as you recognize the beginning of your opponent's technique, aim a quick jab to your opponent's head. Ensure that you stretch your arm and transfer your weight to the front. In training, the palm of the hand should be hit toward your partner's chest to avoid injury.

This countertactic can be used against a knee technique with the right leg (photos 126 and 127) and against a technique with the left leg (photo 128).

Photo 126   Photo 127   Photo 128

Step and Hook

This countertactic is used against a straight knee kick from a distance.

For protection against this technique, perform a quick step to the inside, concurrently turning your body sideways to your opponent. At the same time, throw a jab or hook to his or her head.

In photos 129 and 130, the fighter in red counters against a knee kick with the left leg. For defense against a knee kick with the right leg, the red fighter must put his right foot sideways to the front and punch with his right arm.

Photo 129

Photo 130

Block with Knee

This countertactic is used against a straight knee.

As soon as you recognize the beginning of your opponent's attack, turn slightly and kick with your knee from the inside to the lower area of his or her thigh. For this technique, do not be too close to your opponent and pay attention to a raised guard, as you may otherwise be hit by a punch technique.

Photos 131 and 132 show the countertactic against a kick with the right knee. In photo 133, you can see a kick with the left knee.

Photo 131   **Photo 132**   **Photo 133**

◉ Chapter 8

Countertactics in Clinch Situations

Countering a Knee Kick from the Side

Turn of the Hip and Knee Kick

This countertactic is used in clinch situations against a knee kick from the side.

Turn your hip and move into your opponent. This way you will be hit by the thigh and not by the knee, which results in less impact. If your opponent kicks with his or her left leg, turn to the left (photo 134). If he or she attacks with the right leg, turn to the right. Subsequently, counter with a knee kick to your opponent's lower ribs, using your knee on the side that has been attacked. If your opponent, for example, carries out a kick with his or her right knee, turn your body to the right, then back again, and immediately counter with your left knee.

Photo 134

Photo 135

In photo 135, the fighter in red turns to the right and moves his left leg to the front. This is unnecessary, as his opponent is very close in a clinch.

Countering a Series of Kicks from the Side

Throw to the Side

This countertactic is used in a clinch situation against a series of lateral knee kicks.

If you foresee the beginning of your opponent's knee kick at an early stage, you can use this countertactic with particular success if your opponent uses a number of lateral knee kicks, as can frequently be observed in Thai stadiums. This way, your opponent will tire and can no longer clinch and push as hard as before, which facilitates a throw.

In photos 136 and 137, the fighter in blue tries to deliver a lateral kick with his left leg. The fighter in red recognizes this technique at an early stage and throws his opponent in the direction of the kick.

Photo 136   **Photo 137**

Countering a Grip from Below

Elbow

This countertactic is used in clinch situations when you have an inside hold around your opponent's neck and he or she then attempts to come into this position by raising a hand from below the head.

Defend your position by a hitting-down elbow aimed at the unprotected part of your opponent's head.

In photos 138 and 139, the fighter in blue grips from below with his left hand. The fighter in red defends his position by delivering a hitting-down elbow with his right arm.

Photo 138

Photo 139

Countering an Inner Grip

Pressure to the Arm and Elbow

This countertactic is used in clinch situations if your opponent has gained a hold around your neck with his or her lower arms.

In order to be able to free yourself from the hold, push your opponent's arm down (photo 140) and then deliver a hitting-down elbow to the unprotected part (photo 141). The countertactic must be quick and surprising. If you have performed the tactic on several earlier occasions, your opponent will watch out for a smaller distance in a clinch situation. Instead, try to get a hold from below, which will enable a counter as previously described.

Photo 140

Photo 141

Push the Arm up and Elbow

This countertactic is used in clinch situations if your opponent has taken his or her grip from the inside.

Loosen this grip by quickly pushing up one of your opponent's arms (photo 142). To this end, you must get ahold of his or her elbow and give a firm push. At the end of the move, your opponent's face will be unprotected and you can deliver a hitting-down elbow (photo 143).

Photo 142

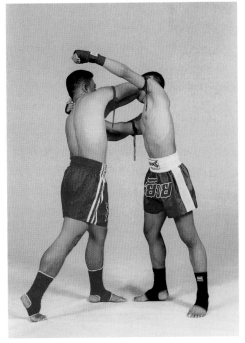

Photo 143

Countering a Close Hold around the Body

Release by Turn of the Body

This countertactic is used in clinching if your opponent is holding you with a firm grip around your chest and is pulling you forcefully to his or her body.

To succeed in a release from this position, perform a turn and raise your inner arm into the air (photo 144). It will now be easier for you to breathe, and you will gain a certain amount of room. This provides you with the opportunity for a hit to your opponent's neck or shoulder from above (photo 145). Then push your opponent away with your lower arm at his or her neck and deliver a knee kick.

Photo 144

Photo 145

Countering a Taller Opponent

Lift and Throw to the Side

This countertactic is used in an infight against a taller opponent.

Grab your opponent around the waist, pull your opponent close to you and lift him or her up (photo 146). To this end you must apply pressure to the upper part of the body, so that he or she will have difficulty breathing and won't be able to deliver an elbow technique from above. Subsequently, push your opponent hard toward the ground, which will cause him or her to lose balance. Promptly throw your opponent to the side (photo 147).

Photo 146

Photo 147

Pressure to the Body

This countertactic is used in clinching against a taller opponent.

If your opponent attempts to put his arms around your neck, grab him or her with both hands around the rib cage and place both your hands above each other at your opponent's back. As an alternative, lock your own elbows, thereby stabilizing the position. Apply firm pressure to your opponent's ribs, so that he or she will have difficulty breathing. Then deliver a blow with your knee to your opponent's thigh, stomach, or lower ribs. In addition, you can push your chin onto your opponent's shoulder or, in the case of a very tall opponent, your head from below to his or her chin.

Photo 148 shows the fighter in blue using this technique. Subsequently, he raises both arms with his elbows in front. In this way, the fighter in red is unable to use his arms and the upper part of his body is not protected against another knee kick (photo 149).

Photo 148

Photo 149

Photo 150: Adisak Dungyai, Fighter name: Nonbee Kiety-ongyuth, Born 1981. Home town: Nakhon Srithamarat province, Approx. 135 professional fights (as of June, 2001), Former Lumpini champion and Rajadamnern champion, (Featherweight)

Controlling Your Opponent

Push Down and Knee

This countertactic is used in a clinch situation if you succeed in getting an inside hold with your lower arms around your opponent's neck and you have placed the palms of your hands above each other on the back of your opponent's head (photo 151).

Control your opponent by moving his or her head abruptly left and right. Then move one leg back and pull his or her head abruptly down (photo 152). Subsequently, deliver a knee kick with your rear leg to the head or body (photo 153).

Photo 151   Photo 152   Photo 153

Step Forward and Throw

This countertactic is used in clinching if you succeed in getting an inside grip around your opponent's neck for control (photo 154).

Starting out from the parallel stance, take one leg forward and push your opponent to the floor.

Photo 155 shows the fighter in blue moving his right leg forward. Subsequently, he throws his opponent to the ground (photo 156).

Photo 154   **Photo 155**   **Photo 156**

Step Back and Throw

This countertactic is used in clinching if you succeed in placing your lower arms from the inside around your opponent's neck.

Control your opponent by moving his or her neck abruptly left and right. Now move one leg somewhat sideways to the front and pull the other leg back, pulling your opponent along and tripping him or her. Subsequently, carry out a knee kick to the head, (a move that an umpire usually tries to stop in fair contests!).

In photos 157 to 159, the fighter in blue moves his right leg forward, pulls the left leg back, and throws his opponent in the process.

Photo 157   Photo 158   Photo 159

Pressure to the Neck with Diagonal Hold

This countertactic is used in clinching. Control your opponent with a diagonal hold around the neck. To this end, you must apply a hold with one arm across his or her shoulder, the other arm below the shoulder, and your hands must be above each other at the back of your opponent's head (photo 160).

Push your opponent a bit to the side, which will leave one side of the body unprotected. Now deliver a knee kick to this area.

In photo 161, the fighter in blue has placed his left arm across his opponent's shoulder and the other arm below the shoulder. He pushes him somewhat to the left side and carries out a knee kick with his right leg to the left side of his opponent's body.

Photo 160

Photo 161

Photo 162: Pornsawan Por Pramook (Lumpini champion) throws Saemsook Por Kaewsaen during clinching. Winner: Pornsawan, Lumpini Stadium, 2000.

Photo 163: Mongkol Karlek, Fighter name: Sakmongkol Sitchoochok, Born: 1973. Home town: Prachinburi province, Approx. 144 professional fights (as of June, 2001), Former Lumpini champion, WMTC champion, (Welterweight)

Part III

Historical Tactics

Photo 164: Densayarm Lukprabat delivers a round kick to the head of Fahpichit Sor Danairit. Winner: Densayarm, Rajadamnern Stadium, 2000.

Chapter 1

Introduction

In the 1950s, major stadiums were built in Thailand. Many spectators visited Thai boxing events, which led to a considerable increase in betting. Enticed by this source of income, the trainers changed their programs so that today's students do not gain a comprehensive athletic background but prepare for fights as early as possible. The athletes receive intensive training only in some basic techniques, until they are able to carry them out by heart, and with power. In the course of a career, a fighter also learns a few additional countertactics, which are particularly suited to his or her style. Moreover, Thailand offers no official trainer education, so anybody and everybody can teach Muay Thai. Against this backdrop, more and more the historical techniques have been forgotten. Now that the sport, considered to be a cultural heritage, enjoys the backing of the Thai authorities both in the professional and amateur areas, the awareness and popularity of the historic techniques is beginning to pick up again. They are now even used in commercials, and sports journals regularly introduce techniques to the public.

Centuries ago, many different styles of Muay Thai were taught and trained. The most well known are the Mae Mai, the Luk Mai, the Chearng and the Kon Muay Thai. The following sections describe the complete set of techniques of the Mae Mai Muay Thai and a selection of very well known Luk Mai, Chearng, and Kon Muay Thai techniques. A comprehensive description of these styles is impossible due to the physical limitations of this book. Differences of opinion regarding the number and execution of techniques also makes this a very difficult task. The names given to these techniques are not translated in English, as they do not describe the contents of the moves and also because of differences in opinion about these techniques. Many Thai and international publications show these techniques without exact descriptions. Depending on the author, frequently they are presented differently, due to a lack of precise information and the fact that each writer uses his or her own sources.

Novices have been injured while practicing a wrong execution. All historical techniques must be subject to a critical examination, and your teachers should be questioned as to their likelihood of success. You should not train for or carry out all the techniques of which you have heard. Otherwise, the danger of injury will cer-

Photo 165: The fighters Sakmongkol Sakchalee and Yordmongkon Sor. Sermngam perform the Corakee Fard Hang technique at a Muay Thai show, Rangsit Stadium, 2000.

tainly outweigh the positive results. It would be advantageous if official Thai sources could end these discussions by introducing a single study program for all historical techniques.

The historical techniques permit concurrent defense and counters. Muay Thai experts like to use them because they are effective and frequently lead to a quick conclusion to a fight. Many of these techniques have been forgotten; I believe an intensive study would be worthwhile. Some of the exercises correspond to basic techniques, which proves that they are still taught in Thai gyms, although not under their original names.

To be a good fighter, you must not master all the following techniques. Many of the current Thai champions do not know how to use a major part of these techniques, or they do not know them at all. It suffices to learn techniques that are easy to practice and execute, and which correspond to your particular skills and talents.

At first, you should train for basic techniques individually and then in combination. Subsequently, you can turn to the countertactics. Once you have mastered these, you can start with the study of the actual historical techniques, as their application is much more difficult and assumes a sound knowledge of basic techniques and countertactics. Thai trainers teach the Mae Mai Muay Thai techniques prior to the Luk Mai, Chearng, and the Kon Muay Thai, as they are considered to be easier to learn and are popular.

Start with a small selection and add others only after these have really been mastered. Before use in the ring, you must be able to deliver these techniques by instinct, as they entail a distinct danger of injury. If, for example, you go down on your knees in defense against a round kick, your opponent may kick from above and make full contact. The historic techniques can be used against attacks from the left and right side of the body. However, the precondition is that your opponent's attack is carried out with force.

Chapter 2

Mae Mai Muay Thai

Salab Fun Phla

This traditional technique is used if your opponent delivers a powerful jab in combination with a forward motion, or a straight punch.

For protection against the attack, take a half circle to the outside. At the same time, push your opponent's upper arm away with your front hand and pull his or her lower arm toward you with your rear hand. The technique could break your opponent's arm.

In photo 166, the fighter in blue delivers a straight punch with his right arm, which the fighter in red tries to avoid with a step to the outside left. If the punch is carried out with the left arm, the defending fighter must step to the right.

Photo 166

Paksa Waeg Rang

This traditional technique is used against a powerful jab accompanied by a step to the front or a straight punch.

   As soon as you detect the beginning of the blow, take a step forward and turn the upper part of your body slightly toward your opponent's arm. In the process, block with the arm opposite to your opponent's technique and deliver an uppercut elbow to the head. Some trainers teach the technique so that both lower arms are directed from the inside toward the opponent's punch arm while keeping the arms about 20 centimeters apart. The elbows will be somewhat wider.

   In photo 167, the fighter in red defends himself against a technique with the right arm. If the opponent delivers the technique with the left arm, he must turn his body to the right and strike with the left elbow.

Photo 167

Chawa Sad Hok

This traditional technique is used against a powerful jab accompanied by a step to the front or a straight punch.

As soon as you detect the beginning of the punch, bring your front foot forward to the side so that your opponent's attack misses the target. In the process, bend your front leg and shift your weight to this leg. At the same time, deliver a cutting elbow to your opponent's ribs or the solar plexus.

If your opponent hits with his or her right arm, move your front leg forward to the left and hit with your right elbow (photo 168). If your opponent uses his or her left arm, move your front leg forward to the right and strike with your left elbow.

Photo 168

Inao Tang Grid

This traditional technique is used against a powerful jab accompanied by a step forward or a straight punch.

As soon as you detect the beginning of the punch, promptly move your front foot forward to the side so that your opponent's technique misses the target. In the process, bend your front leg and transfer your weight to this leg. At the same time, deliver a cutting elbow to your opponent's ribs or solar plexus.

If your opponent punches with his or her right arm, move your front leg forward and sideways to the right and strike with your left elbow (photo 169). If, however, your opponent uses his or her left arm, your front leg must be moved forward sideways to the left and the hit delivered with your right elbow.

Photo 169

Yok Kow Pra Sum Erru

This traditional technique is used against a powerful jab accompanied by a step to the front or a straight punch.

As soon as you detect the beginning of the technique, bend your legs so that the punch misses your head. Then counter from a distance with an uppercut to the chin while stretching your legs for a strong execution of the technique.

In photo 170, the fighter in red uses the technique against a punch with the right arm. For a punch with the left arm the defending fighter must adopt the conventional stance and hit with his right arm. To this end, the fighter on the photo must change his stance by pulling his left leg back or by a very quick forward move of his right leg.

Photo 170

Ta Then Kam Fak

This traditional technique is used against a powerful jab accompanied by a step to the front or a straight punch.

Once your opponent starts his or her technique, take a step to the front, bend your front leg, and transfer your weight to this leg. In addition, the upper part of your body can slightly lean to the side. In the course of your forward move, push your opponent's punch upward with your opposite lower arm. Subsequently, you can deliver a technique with your other arm or a knee kick to the unprotected part of your opponent's body.

In photo 171, the fighter in red defends himself against a punch with the right arm. For defense against a left arm he must block with his right lower arm. If, in the process, he moves his right leg to the front, he can deliver a forceful hit with his left arm.

Photo 171

Morn Yan Lak

This traditional technique is used against a powerful jab accompanied by a step to the front or a straight punch.

Once you detect the beginning of the punch, promptly carry out a front kick to the solar plexus or the stomach. Your opponent should lose his or her balance and fall back. You can then follow up with other techniques such as a round kick with the other leg.

In photo 172, the fighter in red defends himself against a punch with the left arm. If he is attacked with the right arm, he must use his right leg for the technique.

Photo 172

Pak Look Toy

This traditional technique is used against a round kick to the body or head.

As soon as you detect the beginning of the kick, move your outer foot somewhat more to the outside, followed by your other foot. In the process, turn in the direction of the kick and deliver a strike with your front elbow to your opponent's leg. Some trainers prefer the delivery to the shinbone, however, as it is very hard. The attack as shown can also be aimed at the thigh, slightly above the knee.

In photo 173, the fighter in red defends himself against an attack with the right leg. In contrast to the photo, many fighters move the right foot forward for a more forceful delivery of the blow with the elbow. If your opponent kicks with his or her left leg, you must make a forward step to the left, turn to the right, and make a subsequent strike with the left elbow.

Photo 173

Chorakee Fard Hang

This traditional technique is used if a round kick has missed the opponent.

Promptly move your leg back and deliver a hit with your heel to your opponent's head. The technique is also possible if your opponent carries out a powerful straight punch. Then take a step to the outside, so that the punch misses the target and your opponent loses his or her balance. Thereafter, deliver a kick to the unprotected area of your opponent's head, using the leg opposite to your opponent's punch.

In photo 174, the fighter in red aims his right leg from left to right to his opponent's head. Prior to that move, he used this leg for a round kick that missed the target. As an alternative, he could also turn 360 degrees and use the momentum for a powerful hit with the leg.

Photo 174

Hak Ngoang Aiyara

This traditional technique is used against a round kick to the ribs.

As soon as you detect your opponent's technique, take a step away from the kick to the outside and grab the kick. This is quickly followed by delivering a hit from above with the elbow of your front arm to your opponent's thigh. In addition, you may raise the leg and unbalance your opponent. If you strike without catching the leg, you are in less danger of being hit by the kick.

In photo 175, the fighter in red stops the kick and hits with his elbow to the thigh. If, in contrast to the photo, he attacks from below, the leg can be pushed up. This risks the leg sliding along his arm and hitting his head. Many fighters take a bigger step forward than the one pictured on the photo, as this gives them more time to catch the kick and deliver a more powerful blow with the elbow.

Photo 175

Nakha Bid Hang

This traditional technique can be used against a front kick or a round kick.

To stop your opponent's technique, take one step back. In the process, seize your opponent's heel with one hand and the toes of his or her foot with the other, and promptly turn them up. Thereafter, carry out a knee kick to your opponent's calf or thigh. With boxing gloves, it is difficult to catch the foot, which is why this technique is better suited for self-defense and is not recommended for athletic contests.

In photo 176, the fighter in red has taken hold of his opponent's leg and pulls it back. This will have an effect similar to turning up the front of the foot.

Photo 176

Viroon Hog Glab

This traditional technique is used against a round kick to the body or head.

As soon as you recognize the beginning of the kick, deliver a quick front kick with your heel to your opponent's thigh. This way, your opponent loses his timing and balance and, after a hard kick, may even be unable to continue the fight.

In photo 177, the fighter in red defends himself against a kick with the right leg. For defense against a kick with the left leg, he must use the left leg.

Photo 177

Dap Chawala

This traditional technique is used against a powerful jab accompanied by a step to the front or a straight punch.

Defend yourself by leaning your body slightly to the left and pushing down your opponent's hitting arm. Use the palm of the hand opposite to the punch. At nearly the same time, counter with a straight punch to your opponent's head.

In photo 178, the fighter in red defends himself against a punch with the right arm. For the defense against a punch with the left arm, the opponent's technique must be deflected to the left and the counter carried out with the left arm.

Photo 178

Khun Yak Jab Ling

This traditional technique can be learned for defense against a quick combination of a punch, kick and elbow.

The fighter in red initially blocks his opponent's straight punch with the raised guard to the outside (photo 179). Thereafter, he defends himself against a round kick by hitting the opponent's thigh with the bone of the elbow (photo 180). Finally he blocks a hitting-down elbow (photo 181) and is now prepared to counter.

Photo 179

Photo 180

Photo 181

Hak Kor Earawan

This traditional technique is used against a powerful jab accompanied by a step to the front or a straight punch.

Deflect your opponent's attack with the opposite hand, downwards and to the outside. Then pull your opponent's head down, seize the unprotected part of his or her neck with your front arm, and deliver a knee kick.

In photo 182, the fighter in red deflects his opponent's punch to the left outside and pulls his opponent's head toward him with his right arm. If the head is pulled down sufficiently, a knee kick can be delivered.

Photo 182

Photo 183: Somlruck Khamsing hits Kamel Jamel (Morocco) with an uppercut elbow. Sanumlung Park, 2000.

Chapter 3

Luk Mai, Chearng, and Kol Muay Thai

Pra Yaikae

This traditional technique originates from the Chearng Muay Thai and is used for an elbow technique to the opponent's head.

Try to irritate your opponent by covering his or her face with the hand of your front arm (photo 184). If you succeed, follow up with a quick hitting-down elbow or cutting elbow with your rear arm (photo 185). As an alternative, you can also push your opponent's front hand to the outside with the subsequent delivery of an elbow technique.

If your opponent moves in your direction, remain in the starting position. However, if he or she remains stationary or steps back, concurrently move your rear leg forward and deliver a strike with your elbow for a more powerful execution.

Photo 184   Photo 185

Kwang Liew Lang

This traditional technique originates from the Luk Mai Muay Thai and is used to keep the opponent at a distance.

If, for example, one of your round kicks has missed its target, promptly move from your position in the direction of your opponent's body or head.

In photo 186, the fighter in red delivers a kick to his opponent's head. Prior to this technique, he carried out a round kick with his right leg and missed the target so that this leg had been on the left before the backward move.

Photo 186

Batha Loob Pak

This traditional technique originates from the Kon Muay Thai and is used for defense against a powerful jab accompanied by a step to the front or a straight punch.

Deflect the punch with the opposite hand to the outside. As an alternative, the upper part of your body may lean back to get out of reach of your opponent's attack. Then carry out a quick front kick with your heel or the entire foot to your opponent's head (photo 187). This is usually done with the rear foot, as this will give you more power and may even lead to a knockout.

Photo 187

Khon Rook Khamoon

This traditional technique originates from the Kon Muay Thai and is used against a high round kick.

When you recognize the beginning of the kick, move forward and kneel down. With one hand, grab your opponent's heel. With your other hand, seize his or her thigh (photo 188). Right after the kick has passed above your head, quickly stand up and pull along your opponent's leg at the joint of the foot. At the same time, push the thigh away, which will lead to a hard fall.

It is difficult to carry out the Khon Rook Khamoon with boxing gloves, so this technique is recommended for self-defense and not for a contest.

Photo 188

Monto Nang Tak

This traditional technique originates from the Kon Muay Thai and is used against a round kick to the body or head.

As soon as you recognize the beginning of the kick, jump toward your opponent as if you were going to sit on his or her thigh. Then the kick will have no impact. In the course of the jump, deliver an elbow to your opponent's face.

Photo 189 shows this technique against a kick with the left leg. If the opponent attacks with the right leg, the fighter in red must move his left leg forward and deliver the blow with his left arm.

Photo 189

Hak Lak Ped

This traditional technique originates from the Kon Muay Thai and is used against a front kick.

Once you recognize the beginning of the kick, jump back so that the technique misses its target. In the process, catch the kicking leg with one hand at the heel and the other hand at the toes. Push the leg down, quickly position one leg on top, and sit down with all your weight. Keep holding the foot with your hands; this will overstretch, or even break, your opponent's leg.

If your opponent kicks with his or her right leg, capture the heel with the right hand and the toes with the left hand. The turn is carried out to the left. If the kick comes from the right leg, the heel is grabbed with the left hand, the toes with the right hand, and the turn will be to the right.

In photos 190 and 191, the fighter in red turns to the left with his right hand raised. This necessitates a change in hand position and complicates the technique.

Photo 190

Photo 191

Hanuman Fad Kumpan

This traditional technique originates from the Kon Muay Thai and is used against a high front kick.

Once you recognize the beginning of the kick, lean the upper part of your body somewhat back so that the kick misses its target. Grab the kicking leg with one hand at the heel and the other hand at the toes. Now, raise the leg and pull it down across your shoulder. The move must be carried out with force so that your opponent falls down.

If your opponent kicks with his or her right leg, you must grab the heel with your right hand, the toes with your left hand, and carry out the turn to the left (photos 192 and 193). If the fighter kicks with his or her left leg, you must grab the heel with your left hand, the toes with your right hand, and carry out the turn to the right.

Photo 192

Photo 193

Ramasul Kwang Kwoan

This traditional technique originates from the Kon Muay Thai and is used against an opponent with a firm and high guard who is moving to the front or has lost his or her balance.

Push your opponent's guard down with your front arm, jump up, and throw your rear arm into the air. On your way back down, deliver a powerful elbow to the head (photo 194).

Photo 194

Hanuman Hag Darn

This traditional technique originates from the Kon Muay Thai and embraces the simultaneous use of the elbow and knee.

If your opponent attacks with a powerful jab and a forward step, or a straight punch, deflect the technique with the opposite arm to the inside. Then take a small step forward with your foot on this side of the body to the outside and deliver your elbow and your knee to your opponent's body. The elbow is directed to the head and the knee to the stomach.

Photo 195 shows the technique against a punch with the right arm. If the opponent uses his left arm, the fighter in red must deflect the punch with his right arm to the left. Subsequently, he should take a step forward with his right leg to the outside and use his left elbow and knee.

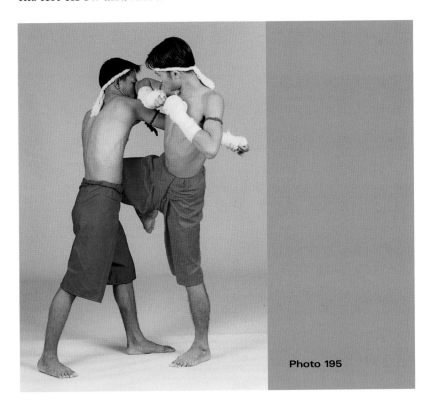

Photo 195

Ega Cheak Rang

This traditional technique originates from the Kon Muay Thai and describes the rapid deflection of the opponent's hands inside out, to open his or her guard.

Jump up and deliver a knee kick to your opponent's stomach (photo 196) or solar plexus.

The technique is most useful if your opponent approaches you or has lost his or her balance.

Photo 196

Part IV

Training
in Thailand

Photo 197: Manja Kietnapachai hits Singdom Or. Aukrit with a round
kick to the head, Lumpini Stadium, 1999.

Chapter 1

Frequently Raised Questions

Athletes with an intense interest in Muay Thai frequently have the desire to experience the martial art in the country of origin, Thailand. Here they will be able to watch the best international Thai boxers in training and actual contests. They will also have the opportunity for a substantial improvement of their own performance level, due to the excellent trainers and training partners available in Thailand. Training in Thai boxing and recreation in the "holiday paradise" of Thailand can be combined. Training in Thailand is also recommended to those followers of Muay Thai who do not have the chance to practice the sport in their home environments. After an intensive course in Thailand, training can be continued at home. I took the opportunity to travel to Thailand as a novice in Muay Thai and to learn the sport thoroughly on site. To achieve this goal, I trained for several months each year at professional martial art gyms. The most often asked questions in respect to my training in Thailand follow, as do their respective answers.

Is Thailand dangerous?
Who do you meet in training?

Thailand is considered to be a fairly safe holiday destination, but as long as you are not familiar with the country, you should avoid some areas, particularly at night. In addition, it is better not to show off with money, as this may provoke theft. If you respect the differences in culture and pay attention to the specific rules of conduct, you will have a wonderful journey. In the course of my frequent travels to Thailand, I have never been robbed and have never observed any such incidents.

The training is attended by a large variety of people, from an Australian lifesaver, to a soldier or a Harvard student. Some athletes try to make money on the professional Thai boxing circuit; others enjoy an extended vacation. Many interested parties train with their own martial arts studio in mind. Muay Thai training is open to many kinds of people.

Photo 198: This group photo with Christoph Delp was taken during training at the Fairtex Gym, Bangkok, 2000.

Are women permitted to participate in training and do age restrictions exist?

Fights between women are becoming more and more popular in Thailand, and a large number of gyms are available for women.

There is no age restriction for participating in training. Even children may train in some of the gyms. Parents should observe the training, at least in the first few days. If you travel by yourself, you have to be at least eighteen years of age. Otherwise, no age restrictions exist. It is recommended that individuals of advanced age select a gym with an international reputation, as these establishments usually offer a higher degree of comfort. Furthermore, the gyms that are regularly attended by foreigners are better prepared to meet the wishes and demands of these customers. For protection against the sun, the training site should have a roof. Nowadays you can even find gyms where the training is conducted in closed buildings.

Is it too hot for training?

The very hot part of the summer in Thailand extends from March to May. Allow ample time for your body to get accustomed to the conditions. Once your body gets used to the climate, you can begin training, even during the hot spell.

Your body will require a few days to make the change. For this reason, never begin intensive training in the first few days after your arrival. The training sessions should be short, even if you have the energy to continue. Otherwise, you will be in danger of falling ill, which could ruin your visit.

Be aware of air-conditioning. Athletes who are drenched in sweat and check into air conditioned rooms are very much at risk of catching a cold.

What other illnesses can be expected?

Diarrhea is the most frequent illness, which is usually overcome in a short time. Hepatitis, rabies, and malaria, illnesses not particularly common in the Western world, are sporadically reported. In addition, attention must be paid to the dangers related to sexually transmitted diseases.

Thailand has poisonous and spiny animals. They rarely attack. Even venomous snakes usually attack only in self-defense.

In order to train in Thailand, how good must I already be in the sport and what are the physical preconditions?

To be able to train in Thai gyms you usually do not have to be in particularly good physical shape. Comprehensive prior knowledge of Muay Thai is not required. Whether or not you will be admitted depends on the respective gym. At some gyms, for example, there are only a small group of highly talented fighters; other gyms are open to anyone interested in Muay Thai.

Photo 199: Master Natchaphol (right) together with the Muay Thai trainer Oliver Glatow, Muay Thai Institute, 2000.

You can also start your training of Muay Thai in Thailand as an absolute beginner. To this end you should, however, plan for a stay of several weeks and not give up after initial minor problems.

If you want to carry out the sport with the same intensity as professional Thai boxers, you must be accustomed to regular training and have a comprehensive knowledge of Muay Thai.

Must I be able to speak the Thai language?

In all tourist centers and the major cities you will be able to get along with English. In rural areas, it is best if you speak a little Thai or have a sufficient number of dictionaries on you. In the course of an extended period of time in Thailand, you will be able to pick up some Thai phrases fairly quickly.

In training, what you need to do is usually demonstrated, so you do not have to understand the Thai language to learn Muay Thai. In addition, trainers who instruct international students on a regular basis speak at least some English.

How long should I stay?

When planning your visit, your deciding factors should be your own preconditions and goals. Beginners will learn the basic techniques after one month of daily training sessions. Advanced athletes should plan a minimum of fourteen days, which will allow sufficient time for your body to get used to being in Thailand.

If you are not necessarily aiming to improve your athletic performance, you can plan the visit as you like. Fights can be seen in the tourist areas at regular intervals and a trainer can easily be found for a separate training session.

Where can I train and how can I book a training session?

Training facilities are available in all cities and tourist centers, as well as in many villages. It is best to ask for a gym near you and follow this up with a visit. If you would like to train in rural areas, it is recommended that you visit one of the major stadiums and speak to one of the trainers.

A stay in one of the major gyms can be booked via the Internet. This is recommended as a first step for beginners. You should not book for an extended period of time, as you will meet many trainers from different gyms on site.

Photo 200 shows Paisitong Jorsambad, Coke, Ningsajam (former Lumpini champion), and Jakid Fairtex, Fairtex Gym, Bangkok, 2000.

How much will the training in Thailand cost?

The rates for training vary. The same club may often charge different fees for similar services, depending on how interested they are in an athlete. If he is considered to be a future fighter, he can train for close to nothing.

International gyms offer fixed rates, which can only be nego-tiated if you are planning to stay for an extended period of time. The total price for training, food, and overnight accommodation is approximately US$30–40 per day.

If you look around on site you will be able to find a trainer for about US$5 per day. Thailand issues no training licenses to native trainers, so it can be difficult to judge their qualities. Therefore, such a search for a trainer can only be recommended to advanced athletes. Novices should first book a course in one of the better-known gyms and look for an appropriate training environment thereafter.

Where can I fight and how much money can I earn?

The best-known stadiums are in Bangkok. Other stadiums can be found in many of the major Thai cities and tourist centers. The respective promoter decides whether an athlete can compete. If you are in a good physical condition, matchmakers will fre-quently speak to you during training sessions.

In comparison to what we are accustomed to, the financial return is very low. A bigger purse can only be won in fights in major Thai stadiums and with live TV coverage. Only a few for-eigners have achieved this; many athletes travel to Thailand merely for training and contests in their home countries.

Photo 201: Wiwat Choo-Ubon, Fighter name: Khunpinit
Kiethawan, Born: 1979. Home town: Pattalung province,
Training camp: Kaew Sumrit, Bangkok, Approximately 126
professional fights (as of June, 2000), Former Lumpini champion, (Featherweight)

◊ Chapter 2

Travel Arrangements

General information

Thailand is part of Southeast Asia and covers an area of 198,404 square miles. To the west and north it borders Burma, Laos to the northeast, Cambodia to the east, and Malaysia to the south. The country can be divided into four topological areas: the southern rain forests and palm beaches, the fertile central section, the mountainous and well-wooded north, and the northeast, with its well-known rice fields.

Thailand has a population of approximately sixty-two million people; nine to ten million of them live in Bangkok, the country's capital. The official language is Thai, but English is understood in the tourist centers and among the authorities of major cities.

The best time for a visit is the fairly dry and cool period from November to February. The hottest period extends from March to May, followed by the rainy season from June to October. However, the rainfall during the season is usually limited to short showers, so Thailand can also be recommended for a visit at that time. Detailed information can be obtained from Thai tourist offices or a travel agent.

The Thai currency is the Baht. Forty Baht correspond roughly to one US dollar, and forty-seven to one Euro. However, in the course of the last years, the Baht has been subject to sizeable fluctuations in the exchange rate. To avoid traveling with large amounts of cash, it is recommended to pay with traveler's checks, Visa, or MasterCard, which are accepted on nearly all occasions.

Visa

A visa is not required for visits up to thirty days. The passport must, however, be valid for a minimum of a further six months. For a tourist visa (up to sixty days) or a nonimmigrant visa, contact one of the Thai diplomatic representatives. In Thailand, a visa can be extended by fifteen days or by thirty days after a border crossing and return on the next day.

Thai Representations in the USA

Royal Thai Embassy
1024 Wisconsin Avenue, N.W.
Suite 401
Washington D.C. 20007
Tel.: (202) 944-3600
Fax: (202) 944-3611
www.thaiembdc.org

Royal Thai Consulate-General
700 North Rush Street
Chicago, IL 60611
Phone: (312) 664-3129
Fax: (312) 664-3230
Thaichicago@aol.com

Royal Thai Consulate-General
351 East 52nd Street
New York, NY 10022
Phone: (212) 754-1770
Fax: (212) 754-1907
Thainycg@aol.com

Royal Thai Consulate-General
611 North Larchmont Boulevard,
Second Floor
Los Angeles, CA 90004
Phone: (323) 962-9574
Fax: (323) 962-2128
www.thai-la.net
thai-la@mindspring.com

Thai Representations in Canada

Royal Thai Embassy
180 Island Park Drive
Ottawa, Ontario
Phone: (613) 722-4444
Fax: (613) 722-6624

Thai Representations in the UK

Royal Thai Embassy
29 - 30 Queen's Gate
London, SW7 5JB
Phone: (44-20) 789-2944
Fax: (44-20) 782-9695

Travel information

In the USA and Canada

Tourism Authority of Thailand
611 North Larchmont Boulevard
First Floor
Los Angeles, CA 90004
Phone: (323) 461-9814
Fax: (323) 461-9834
tatla@ix.netcom.com

Tourism Authority of Thailand
c/o World Publications
304 Park Avenue South
Eighth Floor
New York, NY 10010
Phone: (212) 219-4655
Fax: (212) 219-4697
tatny@aol.com

In the UK

Tourism Authority of Thailand
3rd Floor, Brook House
98 - 99 Jermyn Street
London SW1 Y6EE, England
Phone: (44-207) 925-2511
Fax: (44-207) 925-2512
info@tat-uk.demon.co.uk

In Thailand

TAT Head Office:
(Tourism Authority of Thailand)
4 Ratchadamnoen Nok Avenue
Bangkok 10100
Phone: 02/2810422
Fax: 02/2246221
info@tourismthailand.org
TAT offices can be found in all of
the major tourist centers.

Customs regulations

Only one photo or video camera may be imported, but this is rarely checked. In addition, you may bring along tax-free spirits up to 1 liter, two hundred cigarettes, and perfume for your personal requirements. When importing medicine it must be ensured that the components are not subject to the strict Thai drug legislation. The export of Buddhist statues too big to carry on your body is forbidden. Antiques may only be taken out of the country with a special permit.

Comprehensive information on all customs regulations is available at all Thai tourist offices.

Photo 202: Somkid Kruewaan, Fighter name: Terdkiat Sitteppitak/Kietrungroj, Born: 1970. Home town: Buriram province, Approximately 150 professional fights (as of June, 2001), Training camp: Kietrungroj Gym, Rayong province, Former Lumpini champion (Junior featherweight, Featherweight and Junior lightweight) and WMTC champion.

What Should Be Taken Along?

- **One set of proper clothing.** If you visit a Thai government authority you must be properly dressed. This is also recommended for all official functions and invitations. Otherwise you only have to take along the bare necessities, as clothing can be purchased in Thailand at a favorable price.

- **Diarrhea medication, insect repellent, suntan lotion, and prophylactics**. These should be taken along as a precautionary measure. Large supplies are not required as all of these products are readily available at numerous Thai pharmacies.

- **Credit cards (Visa/MasterCard) and traveler's checks (American Express).** Visa and MasterCard can be used at cash dispensers and in shops. They are not only a means of payment but are also best suited for the withdrawal of cash. However, cash machines can often be out of service for a number of days, so it is best to carry traveler's checks for this purpose.

- **Important telephone numbers and addresses.** Important telephone numbers and addresses that you should have on you are these of your diplomatic representatives (as listed below), the head office of Thai tourist information, your travel agent, and your airline.

- **Copy of your passport and flight ticket.** Keep a copy of your passport and keep it separate from the original. This will enable your embassy to issue a temporary passport without much delay if the original should be lost or mislaid. If you lose your flight ticket, you will need a copy to present to the airline.

- **Mouth guard.** It is difficult to buy a mouth guard in Thailand. Some of the fighters do not wear a guard, which is certainly not recommended, on account of possible injuries.

Important Addresses in Thailand

In the case of an emergency, if you are looking for an English-speaking doctor, or you have been robbed, contact your embassy.

United States Embassy
120/22 Wireless Road
10330 Bangkok
Phone: 02/2054000

British Embassy
1031 Wireless Road
10330 Bangkok
Phone: 02/2530191

Canadian Embassy
15th Floor, Abdulrahmin Place
990 Rama IV Road
10500 Bangkok
Phone: 02/6360560

Medical Services

Thai practitioners are usually well educated. However, if you fall ill, you will have to bear the fees charged by private hospitals. For this reason, make sure you are covered by a corresponding health insurance before traveling to Thailand. To be able to claim the hospital charges at home, you must get a receipt, as far as is possible in English. Such travel insurance is usually offered by the majority of insurance companies at reasonable cost.

Dangers and Annoyances

Tourists can easily contract mild attacks of stomach and bowel illness at the beginning of their visit. These can usually be overcome quickly with common medication such as Imodium. To avoid these maladies, do not buy any food from vendors on busy roads or from stands presenting the food without a cover. It is recommended to boil tap water before drinking it and not to consume ice cubes or raw food products.

The necessity of a malaria prophylaxis depends on your destination. For most of Thailand it is not required. However, a few weeks before departure, try to get advice on the current situation from an institute for tropical diseases or the Thai Tourist Office. In any case, you should protect yourself against mosquito bites, which can lead to dengue fever.

Thailand has a large number of people suffering from AIDS. Protection is mandatory for all sexual contacts.

Bites by dogs, cats, or other warm-blooded animals present the danger of rabies. If you have been bitten, you should promptly seek medical attention, even though the wound may be small.

If you are stung by a scorpion or bitten by a snake or spider, you should be able to describe the animal as closely as possible to enable the doctor to select the correct serum. For protection against these injuries, wear sturdy boots, particularly in a rain forest.

The sale or possession of drugs is punishable by a severe prison sentence, and possibly even the death penalty. Prior to arrival or departure, particular attention must be paid to your luggage. If you are not quite sure, check again. Packages from strangers must not be taken along.

Attacks on tourists are rare. To lower the risks even further, do not visit secluded areas alone and abstain from walks in unknown suburbs at night. For protection against muggings, avoid wearing precious and flashy jewelry and showing off with money.

The hotel safes are normally quite reliable. To avoid a misuse of your credit cards, do not leave them behind in smaller hotels.

Conduct in Thailand

The interpersonal relationships in Thailand differ somewhat from those in Western countries. The following rules of conduct should be adhered to strictly.

The royal family and the monks enjoy very high regard and may never be criticized or offended.

You may never touch the head of other people, including children. This is considered an insult, as Thais consider the head to be the seat of the soul. You must also keep away from touching casual acquaintances of the opposite sex. This would cause embarrassment for that person.

You should never raise your voice or show anger, as such conduct is interpreted as weakness ("loss of face"). If you raise your voice or bellow in a conflict situation, you may make a fool of yourself. Speaking in a loud voice is generally considered to be impolite.

Thais regard the feet as impure. The feet must not be pointing in anybody's direction; they must not be held high, and, when you are seated, they should not be aimed at the person in front of you. Additionally, you may not step across individuals lying on the ground. When entering a temple or a flat, remove your shoes.

Thais attach great importance to smart clothing and expect foreign visitors to do the same. Anyone who, in spite of this, wears old or dirty clothes will be regarded as a beggar and a tramp and will be treated disrespectfully. Furthermore, no provocative clothing should be worn. For example, women should not wear clothes with low necklines or very short skirts, because only prostitutes dress this way in Thailand.

The greeting with a Wai must be acknowledged. This is inappropriate for beggars, who may consider it as derisive.

By and large, all people should be treated with courtesy and respect. If somebody smiles at you, reply with a smile of your own.

More information on visits to Thailand can be gathered from the Lonely Planet travel guide to Thailand.

◊ Chapter 3

Selecting a Gym

The search for a trainer and a gym should be conducted with particular care, as the final choice will have a decisive influence on your athletic development.

If you plan a short visit to Thailand, you should train in one of the internationally reputed gyms. These gyms are accustomed to foreigners; the staff is able to communicate in English; and the athletic requirements are known. However, the training fees are usually fairly high, and foreign and Thai boxers are frequently separated. A close relationship with the trainer, as is normally the case in Muay Thai, does not always develop.

If you wish to spend more time in Thailand for training, you should initially visit some of the gyms before you make a decision. Gyms and a large number of trainers can be found in nearly all villages and towns. For your final selection, you can first determine a venue and then look for a suitable training facility in the neighborhood.

As an alternative, you can also go to boxing events, and, if you like a fighter's technique, ask his trainer about the location of his club and whether you might be permitted to join. The comfort and equipment of these gyms often cannot be compared to international standards, but it will offer you the opportunity to gain inside knowledge of the sport. The charges are considerably lower than the ones you can expect in internationally reputed clubs.

If a manager sees a foreign athlete as a potential source of income, the athlete will be expected to pay low, or no, fees. Needless to say, you first have to train hard enough to be accepted as an athlete by fighters and trainers alike.

Only a few particularly talented sportsmen may train in specialized gyms. The managers of these gyms employ the best trainers and acquire the latest training equipment in order to nurture the sportsmen in the best way possible to develop into top athletes. Sportsmen with low levels of fitness are not encouraged to train at the same time in such gyms and thus prevent the trainers from working with the more talented competitors.

Photo 203 shows the boxer Menny Ossi, Master Chalee (several-time Lumpini champion), Mr. Fitzgerald (professional umpire) and Christoph Delp at the Muay Thai Institute, 1999.

More details on Muay Thai can be found on the Internet pages of Ralf Kussler (www.hanuman-camp.de) and Christoph Delp (www.muaythai.de, www.thaisport.de).

Glossary

The following is a listing of the best-known basic Muay Thai techniques, first listed in English, and then in Thai. They are comprehensively described in the book Thai-Boxen basics (Delp, 2001).

Fist Techniques

- **Hook punch** (mat hook, mat weang sun): Lateral punch with the arm kept nearly parallel to the ground.
- **Jab punch** (mat jab, mat throng chock num): Straight punch technique with the front arm.
- **Straight punch** (mat throng, mat throng chock tam): Straight punch technique with the rear arm.
- **Swing** (mat weang yao, mat kwang): Lateral punch technique with a wide swinging motion.
- **Uppercut** (mat ngad, mat seri): Punch technique carried out from below with the arm held at an angle.

Elbow Techniques

- **Cutting elbow** (sok tad): Lateral elbow technique with the hitting arm held horizontally.
- **Elbow cuff from above** (sok sub): Elbow from far above, often in the process of a jump.
- **Hitting-down elbow** (sok tee): Diagonal elbow technique from above, for which the elbow must initially be turned up.
- **Lift-back elbow** (sok kratung): Elbow to the back from below.
- **Reverse elbow** (sok glab): Elbow technique in the process of a turn.

- **Spear elbow** (sok pung): Diagonal blow with the elbow from above, for which the elbow must first be raised slightly.
- **Uppercut elbow** (sok ngad) = elbow technique from below.

Leg Techniques

- **Continued kick** (te kod, na ca bid hang): Semicircular kick slightly above the target, pulled down shortly before the impact.
- **Half-shin half-knee kick** (te khrung khang khrung khow): Kick with the knee and the shinbone from a close distance.
- **High round kick** (te sung, te karn koa): Semicircular kick to the head or shoulder.
- **Kick from above** (te kook): Kick from above for which the leg is first pushed high in the air.
- **Round kick to the body** (te lam toa, te tad glang): semicircular kick to the body, usually in the direction of the lower rib.
- **Round kick to the leg** (te ka, te tad lang): Semicircular kick to the inside or outside of the leg.

Foot Techniques

- **Back kick** (teeb glab lang, teep yan lang): Kick to the back. The knee is first pulled in, which is followed by the leg to the target area.
- **Ball-of-foot front kick** (teep ruk): Quickly executed forward kick with the ball of the foot.
- **Jab kick** (teep robgaun): Rapid kick, frequently to the legs, to disturb the opponent's timing.

- **Sidekick** (teep khang, teep sakad): Lateral kick with the knee pulled in. In contrast to other types of martial arts, the body is not fully turned to the side.
- **Straight front kick** (teep trong): Powerful forward kick with the entire foot or the heel.

Knee Techniques from a Distance

- **Continued kick** (khow kod): Diagonal knee kick from above, for which the knee must first be raised.
- **Diagonal knee** (khow chiang: Lateral knee kick.
- **Flying knee** (khow loy): Straight knee kick in combination with a jump.
- **Round knee** (khow khong): Knee technique delivered in a circle from the outside.
- **Straight knee** (khow trong): Straight knee kick.

Knee Techniques in Clinch Situations

- **Grab knee** (jab koe tee khow): Knee kick from the front or the side in combination with a hold of the opponent's neck.
- **Knee kick with little force** (khow noi): Knee kick with little power from the outside to the thigh, to disturb the opponent's timing.
- **Lock body knee** (goad aew tee khow): Knee kick from the front or side in combination with a hold of the lower ribs.

Bibliography

Cummings, Joe, Sandra Bao, Steven Martin, China Williams. *Thailand Travel Guide,* 10th edition. Melbourne, Australia: Lonely Planet Publications 2003.

Delp, Christoph. *Thai-Boxen basics.* Stuttgart, Germany: Pietsch Verlag, 2001.

——. *Bodytraining für Zuhause basics.* Stuttgart, Germany: Pietsch Verlag, 2002.

——. *So kämpfen die Stars.* Stuttgart, Germany: Pietsch Verlag, 2003.

——. *Muay Thai: Traditionen, Techniken, Grundlagen.* Stuttgart, Germany: Pietsch Verlag, 2004.

Krack, Rainer. *Thailands Süden.* Bielefeld, Germany: Reise Know-How Verlag, 2000.